GOOD NEWS FOR THE BAD NEWS BLUES

**EVERYTHING IS OKAY
IN A NOT OKAY
SORT OF WAY**

GOOD NEWS FOR THE BAD NEWS BLUES

EVERYTHING IS OKAY IN A NOT OKAY SORT OF WAY

STEVEN EVETTS

First published in paperback in 2020 by Sixth Element Publishing
on behalf of Steven Evetts

Arthur Robinson House
13-14 The Green
Billingham TS23 1EU
Tel: 01642 360253
www.6epublishing.net

© Steven Evetts 2020

ISBN 978-1-912218-96-7

British Library Cataloguing in Publication Data. A catalogue record for this book is available from the British Library.

All rights reserved. No part of this publication may be reproduced, stored in a retrieval system or transmitted, in any form or by any means, electronic, mechanical, photocopying, recording and/or otherwise without the prior written permission of the publishers. This book may not be lent, resold, hired out or disposed of by way of trade in any form, binding or cover other than that in which it is published without the prior written consent of the publishers.

Steven Evetts asserts the moral right to be identified as the author of this work.

Printed in Great Britain.

To Rachel.
A flickering light in the midst of darkness.

CONTENTS

Everything Is Not Okay 5
The People's Temple Agricultural Project 7
The Circus In My Head 10
Black Diamond Rattler 12
Audrey Hepburn 14
Memories On The Fire 18
Broadripple Burned 19
I Haven't Been To As Many Places As Johnny Cash 20
The Hollywood Machete Blues 24
Day Off 26
Knock At The Door 28
Absinthe 34
Going Clear 36
Everything's A Little Fucked Up 38
Jay Adams 41
End Of The World 43
Tom Molineaux 44
I Met Ryan Keely At The Comedy Store 48
My Guitar 51
Postcards In The Mail 52
I Don't Want To Die Like Steve McQueen 55
Therapists & Margaritas 57
The Story Of The Bed Bug Blues 59
California Grizzly Bear 64
Smell Of Cigarettes & Sex 65
Changing Seasons 66
The Ballad Of John Tanner 70

Ink On Paper 81
Cocaine 83
Pogo The Clown 85
Everyone Wants To Kill 87
The Old, White, Republican Right, Tight Fisted, ... 90
Short Sighted, Saving The Rich Tonight Blues
'Fore I'm Dead 92
The Cigarette Stoop 93
Isis 102
Rattle-Snakes For Felons 103
Broke 105
Redline Part 1 107
I Wish I Could Meet You For The First Time Again 109
It's Cold On This Barroom Floor 110
Limerence or Muse 112
The Cecil Hotel 113
I Want A Girl With Heroin Eyes 118
A Shakespearean Sonnet 120
Calabasas 121
Mark 16:18 122
Christmas Day In Los Angeles 124
The Devil's Music 126
Untitled #10 132
Oh Sweet Misty 133
Crazy Eyes 134
The Ballad Of Whiskey And Weed 137
Let's Get Stoned 139
The Ghost Of Peg Entwistle 141
The Hollywood No Shoes Blues 143

Heavy Hearts & Empty Glasses 148
Everything Is Okay 149
Joseph Smith 151
The Hooker With A Heart Of Gold 152
Missing People 154
Sadness Is My Shadow 155
California 157
Not Now 164
The Coffee In My Cup Is Cold 165
You Don't Know Me At All 166
It's Been A While Since I've Been 167
To Any Kind Of Church
Christopher Dennis 170
Who Am I Talking To? 173
Heaven's Gate 174
Another Wedding Day 175
Redline Part 2 178
Junkies 179
One Of Those Days 181
Jumbo's Clown Room 185
Street Corner 187
Motherfucker 189
Coffin 191
I Fell In Love In The Musée D'orsay 193
Overworked & Underpaid 196
Down At The Pool Hall 198
Horiyoshi III 205
Dancing With Death 206
I'm Just Figuring This Shit Out Man 207

The Bastards Killed Emmett Till.................................. 209
The Codeine Blues 213
I Don't Want To Fall In Love.. 214
4am Conversations.. 215
Pacino & De Niro 218
Guns Cocaine Whiskey & Weed 221
Shoot 224
The Girl With The Camera At Big Sur 226
Forgotten People 228
The Masterpiece That Never Was................................. 230
Zombies 231
I'm Taking The Last Of Everything.............................. 234
Am I Helping? Am I Hurting?...................................... 236
Livin' Turns To Dyin' 241
The Only Advice I Ever Listened To 243
This Is Not A Test.. 245
Good News For The Bad News Blues 248
A Short Story By Johnny Snyder 257
Good News For The Bad News Blues Cont'd.............. 263

MISSION STATEMENT

Good News for the Bad News Blues is intended to be a warm blanket, a comforting arm, a reassuring look. It is also intended to be an ice bath, a sucker punch and a disturbing glare. Throughout this collection my goal is to remain as ambiguous as possible in places and as obvious as necessary wherever possible. I will also deny all knowledge or accountability wherever misinterpretation is to be concerned.

I believe it uncontroversial to say we live in a crazy world, presuming you are reading these words as an entity of the world, as we understand it. If you happen to be reading this as an outside entity, that exists beyond the human conception of our world then I can only apologize for any possible confusions. But if you are such an entity please feel free to read this as a representation of the dumb-fuckery of human thinking. I will proceed under the assumption that the following words are intended for those living under the confines of our perception of the world. Back to my initial point, this planet, world, universe, as we perceive it is uncertain, scary, unpredictable and beautiful. We can learn about the universe, we can learn about each other but as much as we learn, questions continue to arise. In order to explain the confusion centered around the activity happening amongst humans across the entirety of the earth, I have taken it upon myself to 'eloquently' place a few words in order in an attempt to describe the phenomena, the phenomena of human suffering and human pleasure,

the phenomena of the human experience, the words I have chosen read as follows: *the world seems kind of fucked up.*

Have you ever wondered about traveling back in time? Living in a different decade or perhaps century? I started thinking about a plethora of times I'd wish to inhabit, but they all had something in common, there was always a little something fucked up, sometimes there was a lot that seemed messed up, but up to this day it's safe to say, there's always been something that's a little fucked up.

So, I wrote this book. It is not a political statement. It is not a cure for evil. It is certainly not a recipe for healthy living. I merely took a little time to make a few stories sort of rhyme. I wrote this to tell everyone, everything is fine, despite everything being fucked up all of the time. So please, free your mind and step inside mine. The exit signs are easy to find. If coffee is your thing, fill up a cup. If whiskey is your drink, fill the glass to the brink. If weed is your desire, get yourself higher and roll that joint right up. Make yourself comfortable whichever way makes you feel fine, a chocolate bar, kale smoothie or a fine wine, just take that step inside and I'd like to be the first to welcome you to *The Good News for the Bad News Blues.*

EVERYTHING IS NOT OKAY

I'm here to say
Everything is okay
Well it's not okay
But it's okay
In a not okay sort of way
I'll explain
Have you ever lived on minimum wage?
It's a pain
Some don't even have that
Y'know what I'm saying?
That is not okay
It's easier to lock people away
Than to rehabilitate
Food is thrown away
People don't even empty their plates
And humans are starving today
Everything is not okay
Dictators are obeyed
Citizens are afraid
At some stage Richard Nixon got laid
Everything is not okay
Speech filled with hate
Kids raised with shame
Kardashian reality television fame
Everything is not okay
Climate change
The leaders are all insane

It's a runaway train
An instruction-less game
A daily hurricane
Everything is not okay
Sure we live
And sure we die
I may not be a saint
But I'm an okay sort of guy
As much as I may try
I'd like to be the first to say
I don't have anything figured out
I'm only thinking things through
As I write these words
To share with you
I also have a secret I'd like to share too
I can only live for me
And you can only live for you
Whatever it is we choose to do
It doesn't matter what it is
As long as we are true
I have *Good News*
For anyone
Who enjoys the *Bad News Blues*
Everything is okay
In a not okay
Sort of way

THE PEOPLE'S TEMPLE AGRICULTURAL PROJECT

Don't drink the Kool Aid
Please don't drink the Kool Aid
The Flavor Aid is laced
With valium
Cyanide
And chloral hydrate
Did you hear the death tape?
Babies crying in the background
Victims cheering aloud
But they drank the Kool Aid down
In that murder
Suicide
Massacre
In Jonestown

Why did they do it?
Over 900 people dead
Over 300 hundred of them kids
Well escaping ain't so easy when there's nowhere around
You see it's only the jungle that surrounds
The project in Jonestown
And the cost of leaving was the price of your life
It was the day Leo Ryan was attacked with a knife
That attack he survived
But it wasn't too much longer brave ol' Leo would be alive
The congressman was handed a note
Asking for help

So he started helping people leave
They were still boarding the planes
When the gunshots came
Jones had sent his men
To kill all of them
Especially Ryan
They didn't have much choice in their dyin'
But a few survived
Barely
So Jones announced it was time
To orchestrate the revolutionary mass suicide
He wasn't sure all would willingly abide
He instructed that the children would be the first to die
Once they died
He asked the adults to drink the cyanide
If they tried to run or hide
They'd be injected and were sure to die
They say you can still hear the cries
Where the people's temple used to reside
They say it's a horrible death
Like someone is stealing all the oxygen you have left
Jim Jones said he'd drink the Flavor Aid too
But even that he couldn't do
He saw their pain
And well
Jim Jones was a principled man that never lived by what he said
So he went on to put a bullet through his own head
Supposedly after everyone else was dead

Please don't drink the Kool Aid
The Flavor Aid is laced
With valium
Cyanide
And chloral hydrate
I heard the death tape
Babies crying in the background
Questions being asked and dismissed aloud
Then they were forced to drink the Kool Aid down
In that murder
Suicide
Massacre
In Jonestown

THE CIRCUS IN MY HEAD

A trapeze artist is swinging from ear to ear
There's a tightrope walker without a safety net
A clown sparks the laughter which is all I can hear
A contortionist contorts
A lion roars
There's so much going on
The audience is clapping along
A magician disappears his wife
A knife thrower throws a knife
I'm pinned to a bed
There's a goddamn circus in my head

I'm trying to talk to the ringmaster but he's not around
There's a fire breather breathing fire
There's an elephant walking the grounds
A human cannonball
Stilt-walkers standing tall
There's too much going on
The audience is clapping along
The juggler throws up too many balls
The acrobats are taking too many falls
I feel like the living dead
Welcome to the circus in my head

There doesn't seem to be any kind of admission fee
Everyone makes their way to their seats freely
Even though I'm supposed to be in control of the show
I guess I can't decide who stays or goes
It had been a while since anyone sat in her seat
But I guess it was me who always kept it free
The seat remained empty
But I heard that she needs tickets for three
I heard you were married
And eventually
The time comes
To take the young ones
To the circus too
So I saved seats for all three of you
Pour me some hundred proof
Light me one up to forget the truth
Let me turn off the lights to the tent
The show must come to an end
I'm the only one paying any rent
I'm raising my glass to
The circus in my head

BLACK DIAMOND RATTLER

I've been living over Beachwood Canyon way
Depending on the temperature during the day
I tend to hang back in the shade
I blend into the surroundings
When those hikers see me they sure seem afraid
When the sun starts to fade
It might be time to catch my prey
But I don't need to eat everyday
I can kill a man or so they say
But the anti-venom normally manages to save
I'm never trying to inflict any pain
I was hoping my rattle would help him stay away
But no
He wanted to play
Pick me up with a stick
Which is not okay
I was minding my business on the ground that I lay
I bet this is y'alls first time in LA
I mean
Have they never seen a rattlesnake?
I was moving around so they knew I wasn't dead or fake
But he soon realized his mistake
I never did bite to pierce skin for the sake
I waited for the venom to take
And needless to say
His friend didn't hesitate
To drag him away

Don't worry I'm sure he was okay
Just might not hike up Beachwood again

I ain't worried about that dumb ass sucker
I'm a crotalus oreganus helleri
Black Diamond Rattler Motherfucker

AUDREY HEPBURN

I fell in love with Audrey Hepburn
So I was obviously sad to learn
That we would never be
Considering she died in 1993
When I turned on the TV
Miss Hepburn I did see
But she wasn't called that on the screen
People were calling her Holly Golightly
I didn't really pay attention to the story
Figured I could read the book
I was too busy falling in love
It must have been a double feature
Because right after
Another movie they played
By the name of *Charade*
Expect the unexpected they say
After seeing this
I was convinced
I don't want to give the story away
But Cary Grant seemed a lucky son of a bitch
I was hoping that maybe one day
Audrey Hepburn would know my name
When I heard the news
I was brought to my knees
I didn't want to believe
Those movies were made in the sixties
It's now 1993

And well things ain't looking so good
For me and Audrey
So I assembled a team
Built me a time machine
Figured I'd go back in time
I at least had to try
Because I was told you shouldn't deny
True love
There was a love no truer
So I went back to some time ago
Landed myself in Rome
On the set of a movie written by Dalton Trumbo
I decided to give Gregory Peck what for
When he wouldn't tell me which way to go
Said Miss Hepburn had gone home
So I waited till the next day
Security dragged me away
Told me I was crazy
I probably shouldn't have mentioned the time machine
But it was too late
I was thrown out of the gates
So down the block I decided to wait
I mean it must be fate
But I wasn't allowed near the set
I had no regrets
I wasn't going to forget
I fell in love with Audrey Hepburn
I decided to stay in Rome
A few years passed y'know

I became an actor
Didn't think that would attract her
But maybe I'd get a job
On the next film she shot
But I would not
I sucked
I was running out of money
But the sky was pretty clear
All of a sudden I'm knocked off my feet by a small deer
And that's when I finally see her
Standing over me
Saying she's so sorry
"Pippin doesn't normally knock people off their feet"
I said "who the fuck is Pippin?"
She said "Pippin is the deer that forced you into sitting"
I said "I'm not one for quitting"
She said "that makes no sense"
So I told her the full story
Watching *Breakfast at Tiffany's*
In 1993
The double feature
Falling in Love
Annoying Gregory Peck
And being thrown off the set
I told her about the time machine and everything
Told her I bought her a ring
And that our future was destined
She was so sweet
Kissed me on the cheek

Took me by the hand and said "come with me"
And the way she led
Asked if I'd been fed
"We can go eat" she said
Pulled up to this office
Thought to myself this is a strange place
Told me they sold the best pastries
Guy started talking to her
Suppose she would have fans
But they were talking real deep man
I could see her gesturing with her hands
I wanted to walk over to see
But I realized they were talking about me
Maybe she was telling him we were getting married
I don't know
I don't speak Italian
Should have learned before I came to Rome
But how was I to know
I'd be here so long
Audrey walked over to me
Says there's somewhere she needed to be
Signed a napkin and gave it to me
I said I can walk her there
Then two doctors strapped me to my chair
Turns out
Audrey Hepburn doesn't believe in time travel
Which is cool
Neither do I

MEMORIES ON THE FIRE

It's late in the evening
Sure I should be leaving
But I just got this fire to light
I can see the water
I can feel the beach under my feet tonight
I'm thinking about her
I'm thinking about them
Some nights are for forgetting
Some are for remembering
But my memory is a liar
So I'm burning my memories on the fire
One by one
I throw each of them on
Letting each take their turn
As I sit and watch them burn
I can feel her warm glow
I can see her face in the smoke
I'm letting both the good times and the bad times go
Holding on only ever made me grow tired
So I'm throwing my memories on the fire

BROADRIPPLE BURNED

The bar was closing
We were all going our separate ways
Everyone tried to drag me away
But I'm a moth to a flame
I was lost in your arms again
After we drove up the Pacific Coast Highway
I still remember the song you played
Broadripple is Burning
Margot & the Nuclear So & So's
We were looking for a private place to go
Before we pulled over
Found a lifeguard tower
Stayed there a few hours
Shit
We always produced magic
So to see the ghost of our love was tragic
But we made the most of it
Kissing in the morning's mist
The sun eventually would rise
And we would realize
That this isn't something we can begin again
So you went back to him
And I sat listening
To that song
You know the one
Broadripple is Burning

I HAVEN'T BEEN TO AS MANY PLACES AS JOHNNY CASH

We were staggering ourselves down old Thane Road
No taxis to call
So we walked by the water as it flowed
A good chance to talk and confide
Keeping ourselves entertained side by side
She enquired if I'd ever seen such a land
I hadn't
You kind of have to go to Juneau to understand

I've been to a few places man
I've been to way too few places man
I didn't cross the desert but I've been there man
I did breathe mountain air man
And sure
Travel I have had my share man
Maybe one day
I can say
I've been everywhere man

I've been to Reno
Not so much Chicago
Or Fargo
Did see the movie
Minnesota
Always seemed a place I should go
I've been to Portland
Hollywoodland

Little Rock
And New York
Never been to Baltimore
Nor have I set foot in Salvador
Thought about heading to Manila
After watching that thriller
Would be killer

I've been a few places man
More than I can count on my hand man
Smoked a joint in the desert man
Smoked a joint in the mountains man
Traveled a lot or a little I suppose it depends man
I've been to the beginnings and the ends man

Had a friend from Boston
I learned to dance the Charleston
With a girl from Dothan
Had a layover in Washington
Crashed a car in Branson
Drove past Monterey
Wish I could have stayed that day
But I have been to San Francisco Bay
Never been to Spirit Lake
But my way I did make
To old Bear Lake
And the Great Salt Lake
Jet skis for fuck's sake
I've been somewhere man

Wasn't expected to go nowhere man
But my feet felt the desert there man
Hiked a mountain without a care man
Traveling I've had my share but not as much as I care man

Never went to Louisville
Or Knoxville
Always wanted to spend time in Nashville
I want to still
I did have plans until
They were forced to be no more
Been to Bakersfield
And Springfield
Not so much Pittsfield
I've been to Idaho
The great unknown
And dated a girl from Ohio
Briefly lived in Pasadena
Thought about going to Catolina
But I never quite had the right demeanor

I've been some places man
Seen some faces man
In the desert we had some races man
The mountains have faces man
I'm traveling with broken shoelaces man
I've been some places man

I've not been to
Pittsburgh
Gettysburg
Or Parkersburg
I also haven't been to El Dorado
But I spent time in Colorado
I've been to Oklahoma City
Park City
Cedar City
And Salt Lake City
Place was great
Just the popular religion was shitty

I've been somewhere man
I've been nowhere man
Been to the desert there man
Climbed the mountain I dared man
Travel I'm well fared man
I suppose I've been somewhere man

I haven't been to as many places as Johnny Cash
I mean
I've been somewhere man
But he went everywhere man

THE HOLLYWOOD MACHETE BLUES

There's a man with a machete
He's running down the street
He's waving his arms
At every person he sees
People are running in fear
And paths are starting to clear
Police have their sirens sounding
While their squad cars are surrounding
The man doesn't seem to know what to do
So he jacks a car at the drive-thru
He's got *the Hollywood machete blues*
He crashes the car
Before driving too far
The police draw their guns
The man decides to run
Till he has nowhere to go
He raises his weapon
As he starts forward stepping
Towards an officer who falls to the floor
Machete in the air
A second officer shoots
The man is no more
Took his last breath
All because he had *the Hollywood machete blues*
He'd been staying on the streets
Sleeping rough for too many weeks
Said he couldn't handle life on the Boulevard

Sure it's pretty hard
Living next to those Walk of Fame stars
Sleeping bags and piss soaked doorways
The roaring cars driving through their hallways
Living with constant noise
Ignored so much you forgot you had a voice
Imagine
What it must take
To make
A person catch a case
Of *the Hollywood machete blues*

DAY OFF

Let's just take the day off
Do whatever we want
We could travel some place new
Or go to our favorite haunts

Let's just take the day off
Go wherever we wish
An art gallery a museum or the movies
Eat a fine steak or some grilled fish

Let's just take the day off
All day we can spend in bed
Or we could go for an adventure up north
We should spend time together
At least that's what the therapist said

Let's just take the day off
Stop for a happy hour on the way home
After hiking to the Observatory
Just the two of us completely alone

Let's just take the day off
We can have a Bloody Mary brunch
Drink whiskey for dinner
Because we forgot about lunch

I heard you took the day off
Well I took the day off too
I don't know what you decided to do
But I spent most of my day thinking about you

KNOCK AT THE DOOR

There was a knock on my door
But it's not a door
I tended to answer anymore
They knocked again
Shouted to be let in
I thought
I wasn't going to let them in before
So I certainly wasn't going to give in to their demands
They knocked again
Begged to be let in
It could have been a mistake
But the man sounded pretty desperate
Thought it wouldn't take long
Just to see what was going on
Boy
I was wrong
I looked out the peephole
But everything seemed circular
I saw a shadow on the floor
So I opened up my door
There laid a man
No grip left in his hands
A vacant look of regret
And blood all over the carpet
I always think
Maybe if I opened the door sooner
His last words might not have been rumors

There was nothing I could have done
But he might not have died alone

There might be one thing
Throughout my rambling
That may have come to your attention
Which you might think I'd like to mention
Why was it my door
That he came a knocking on
Well
Like always there's a girl
I've said it before
I'll say it again
There's always a girl

Her boyfriend
Well
Let's just say
That still to this day
People fear his family name
They are all known to the law
Not in a way that the law adores
Rumor had it
Just a rumor
I'm not confirming shit
Rumor had it
He had a skill for inflicting pain
The kind where you never breathe again

His girlfriend
The girl in question
Was the sweetest of women
Living a life of pretend
He wouldn't tell her anything
And she didn't want to know
But she'd seen the show
And was well aware of the episode
Did everything she could try
In order to turn a blind eye

They met in high school
They were sweethearts
How so many romances start
He wanted to pursue his dreams
Outside the family business you see
And she was by his side
Both trying to make their way in the world
No more time to hide
But life's tough
And things got pretty rough
Before he decided enough was enough
Money was needed
So to his family he pleaded
To join the family business
So they gave him a test
The body still warm
And the ground still cold
When he was told

The sky was the limit
He was no longer legitimate
At first
Life seemed pretty great
They were in love
Rich and living behind gates
Money was coming in fast
And she didn't want to ask
He didn't want to tell
So it worked out pretty well
But killing people takes its toll
There's only so many times
You can watch the body leave the soul
Eventually it catches up to you
And you lose all sense of the right thing to do
It's about then he started to hit her

She told me
She went from being sweet sixteen
To twenty-three
From being a gangster's slag
To a punching bag
She said to me
The love was gone
Not because it had all gone wrong
Despite the nature of his endeavors
They were richer than ever
But she was too scared to leave
Said she thought her best days had been achieved

Because for the rest of her days
She was going to have to spend them doing whatever he says
I kind of wish
I'm not trying to selfish
But
I kind of wish
She'd told me all of this
Before me and her were naked
In my bed
Just waking up

I don't regret a thing
It just might have made me think
I was in need of a stiff drink
But a truer woman I've never met
And I didn't want her to be someone I forget
So stupidly
I'd see her again
Multiple times
In fact
A few months went by
We continued to try
To figure out a way to escape
That wouldn't escalate
To us both sleeping in graves
But it seemed to no avail
I met him once
That was a pretty close call

But he believed our tales which were pretty tall
At least it seemed
Seemed that he believed
But he soon came after me

There was a knock on my door
But it's not a door
I tended to answer anymore
They knocked again
Shouted to be let in
Made quite some noise
But that helped me recognize the voice
So I looked out the peephole
Everything seemed circular
Sure it was late at night
But I know what the barrel of a gun looks like
So I bent down
Let my shotgun sound
I looked out the peephole
That's when
I saw the shadow on the floor
Never shot a man before
I have to tell you my friends
It's not something I ever want to do again

Ruined my night

ABSINTHE

All you need
Is a glass
And a slotted spoon
Some cold water
And a sugar cube
Oh Absinthe
Wash over me
Sweet anise
And wormwood trees
The ultimate remedy
To relieve
Me of my memories
So pour me two shots
Put the sugar cube on top
Move the spoon across
And let the water pour
Oh Absinthe
The holy trinity
And the *eau de vie*
Alcohol made for me
So pass me some
120 proof fun
Or it could be as strong
As 148 proof
I don't care
I want to drink absinthe like Charles Baudelaire
Drink Absinthe

Like Van Gogh and Edgar Allen Poe
James Joyce
Hemingway
And Pablo Picasso
Oh sweet Absinthe

GOING CLEAR

I want to be clear
I mean I want to go clear
With no fear
I bought all the books
Dianetics
Oh fuck
I became clear
Now I'm clear
Clear L Ron Hubbard made it all up
Oh shit
They have all my secrets
And the capacity to kidnap

Oh Scientology
Oh Scientology

One of many bullshit theologies
And false beliefs
Centered around the monetary
Now I'm clear
I went clear
Clear I need a beer
Clear I need to get out of here
Clear the weight on my shoulders is no lighter
Clear L Ron Hubbard was a science fiction writer
Clear Xenu is make believe
Clear I can rhyme miscarriage

With David Miscavige
But I'm also clear
Before I say any more
I need better lawyers

EVERYTHING'S A LITTLE FUCKED UP

My hot water tap is running cold
My coffee is a couple of hours old
I went back to buy her that ring but it had already sold
I just lit the wrong end of the cigarette I just rolled
I'm not saying I'm down on my luck
I'm just saying everything's a little fucked up

All this walking is hurting my feet
I've stepped on every inch of this street
More people seem to be using it to sleep
Ends keep seeming harder to meet
I'm not saying everything sucks
I'm just saying everything is a little fucked up

Sometimes it's easier to make the hard decision
Occasionally to multiply we might need division
There's nothing but bad news on this television
It's like watching my own demolition
I'm not saying we're shit out of luck
I'm just saying everything's a little fucked up

Did you see the breaking news?
Apparently we're all confused
Despite being right about each of our views
I'm wrong so many times being right becomes an excuse
I'm not saying I totally suck
I'm just saying everyone and everything is a little fucked up

For example
I once
Liked this girl
And she liked me too
All good so far
But she
Had a boyfriend
And he was not me
So nothing happened
But that's not the end of the story
I started dating another girl
But the girl I liked and her boyfriend broke up
Me and the girl I was dating had started to become
Quite serious
Like we had each other's keys
To each of our apartments
Pretty heavy shit
But eventually we broke up
Something to do with my emotional availability
And complete insensitivity
I also apparently "avoid issues"
I don't know
Let's not talk about that
We broke up
But me and the other girl had fallen out of touch
I ran into her in a coffee shop
I bought her coffee
I asked how she'd been
We said a bunch of other things

But what is important is
She was single
I was single
We started to date
After a few weeks she was chasing me down the street
With a switchblade
I was naked
She was crazy
I'm not saying that was the final chapter in our book
We got married
But that's a different story
I'm not saying me and her used up all our luck
I'm just saying everything's a little fucked up

The toast is butter side down on the floor
They keep telling me less is more
Doesn't make sense now didn't make sense before
I suppose that's why there's no whiskey left in the bottle anymore
I'm not saying I'm out of luck
I'm just saying everything's a little fucked up

JAY ADAMS

I want to live free
Like the way Jay Adams rode his skateboard with fluidity
If only it was that easy
To live every moment like you're riding clear and totally breezy
But life doesn't always happen on wheels
And we have to take time to feel
Sometimes feeling's hard to do
Jay Adams certainly seemed to know that too
Trouble seems to follow some people
And it's often pretty easy to be found
Especially for a Z-Boy in Dogtown
We all have ups and we all have downs
I'm not trying to be profound
Just saying we sometimes fall further down
Than some of the others that are around
But as cold as life can be
Especially
With a rebellious carefree
Kind of personality
On that skateboard or surfboard Jay Adams was completely free
If he made a mistake
He would just land the trick another way
No thinking just reaction
Grinding
Sliding

Motherfucking gliding
Vertical action
But dope doesn't ever seem to lose her attraction
Living is hard when you're seeking satisfaction
I know
I've been searching for a while
But I want to live free like that Z-Boy style
Wind in my hair
Not a fucking care
That
Is
How
I
Want
To
Live
I want every second to be
Goddamn
Motherfucking
Cool
I don't want to be anybody's fool
I want live like I'm skating at the Dog Bowl school
Like Jay Adams free on his board in an empty pool

END OF THE WORLD

Champagne flutes clink
What used to float
Has started to sink
This is the precipice
Welcome to the brink
It's no time to blink
Just close those eyes and think
Every beginning ends
Every ending begins
Actors pretend
Singers sing
It's easier to start again
Than to keep continuing
But it's hard to see the beginning
Until it's ending
When the plane's going down
The ocean starts to drown
Riots are beginning
The world seems to be ending
If that's true
Come see me
I'll be on the sidelines bartending
And the drinks will be free

TOM MOLINEAUX

Tom Molineaux was on his way to fight Tom Cribb that day
They say on the morning he ate
A boiled chicken and an apple pie
Then drank half a gallon of beer dry
Made his way to the Shenington Hollow
Ten thousand fans followed
What was about to unfold
Was a bunch of bullshit
If the truth is to be told
You see
Tom Molineaux used to be a slave
Born into slavery in Virginia
In the good ol' U S of A
Started bare knuckle boxing on the plantation
He was beating every slave he was facing
Much to his owner's adulation
After one last fight he was paid $500 and told he was free to leave
It was a rarity to see
A slave walk free
To say the goddamn least
But
Tom Molineaux did just that
The owner wagered a hundred grand
But Molineaux was just happy not to be looking back
He fought free men in New York City

And supposedly
Everyone he fought he beat
So he set sail for England
And was trained by a former slave turned boxer by the name of Bill Richmond
Molineaux was winning fights and keeping fit
He called out a man by the name of Tom Cribb
But Cribb didn't want any of it
Said he was retired
But everyone wanted to see it
Even the goddamn King
Cribb eventually decided to fight
It was a heavy downpour that night
It is worth noting Cribb was white
And let's face it
Back in 1810 England was pretty fucking racist
In the 28th round of the bout
Molineaux knocked Cribb the fuck out
But as Cribb and the ground chose to collide
Cribb's cornerman tried to buy some time
By inventing a crazy lie
Said Molineaux had pistol balls in his hands
Which they didn't find
But they wasted enough time
For the umpire to let them progress to round 29
Despite Cribb being down for longer than the count
Molineaux didn't understand
England wasn't ready for an African-American former slave champion of their land

So fans rushed the cage and broke Molineaux's hand
He still went on to fight in the pouring rain
Both trying to beat each other insane
Molineaux's head was bounced off a ring post
Long before concussions were diagnosed
He got back to his feet but he wasn't on his toes
After 55 minutes
Tom Molineaux
Could fight no more
As the story goes
He drank himself to death by the age of 34
In Galway
Ireland
Not a penny to his name
He'll always be the man who escaped
His tortured fate as a slave
Instead he became
The greatest prize fighter of his day
The people just weren't ready to give a black man that name
I suppose they thought it's okay to let any fight begin
Of course
There's a caveat
The white man must win
Because they weren't ready for a black champion
They both came to fight
But Molineaux was the true champion that night

John Henry Lewis and Jack Johnson
The Brown Bomber Joe Lewis and Iron Mike Tyson
Ezzard Charles a.k.a the Cincinatti Cobra and Sonny Liston
Muhammad Ali and the Gentleman Floyd Patterson
The list of greats continues on
I didn't even mention Spinks
Holyfield
Or Foreman
But the greatest boxer of all time for me
Is the boxer that didn't just fight for accolades
He fought to be free
He did what nobody had done before
Cribb was still on his knees after 30 seconds on the floor
The fight shouldn't have continued
No more punches should have been thrown
But the fight continued to go on
I don't give a fuck
That rainy day
The true champion became
A man by the name
Of
Tom Molineaux

I MET RYAN KEELY AT THE COMEDY STORE

I met Ryan Keely at the Comedy Store
It was a good few years ago
I'd never seen her before
My friend introduced us
Told me she was an actress
Known for her videos of lesbian sex
She was famous all over the internet
I'll be the first to admit
I didn't know any of this
But I was immediately struck
By how pretty she looked
Now it's not like we fucked
But I did look her up
And
Well
She's pretty hot
We were standing outside
Her friend needed to talk to mine
Leaving me and her to talk for a little time
She noted I was English and probably wasn't circumcised
I said she might be surprised
But I thought the conversation was refreshingly alive
I met a lot of people at the Store
But Ryan I wouldn't see there anymore
There was a lot of other people I saw
But her conversation seemed extra raw
But alas

A good few years passed
Memories don't tend to last
I was walking on Ocean Avenue
As I occasionally used to do
That's when I noticed you
Ryan Keely
Walking towards me
But it seemed
She was with her family
Her hair had changed
And I didn't notice her straight away
So I tried a few seconds to place
Where it was from that I recognized her face
She looked at me as if to say
"Don't say hello it's not okay"
But it was in a friendly way
As soon as she'd walked on
It dawned on me where I knew her from
I knew her from that conversation all those years ago
When I was smoking outside the Comedy Store
I'm sure they thought I was just a fan
Just another man
And maybe I am
I looked her up back then
So I looked her up again
She was the girl on girl queen
And apparently
The years keep rolling quietly
Some call it art

Some call it filth
Now she's advertised as the world's hottest MILF
She wasn't the first pornstar I'd met
But she left a memory I won't forget
When I see her I don't just see sex
I see the girl from before
I see the Ryan Keely I met at the Comedy Store

MY GUITAR

My heart was left wide open
Poured whiskey on the wound
Because I was hoping
My guitar wasn't too out of tune

You cut me to my knees
I drank till I had no legs
Oh baby listen to me please
My guitar is no longer playing melodies

I was broken and completely lost
Drank enough liquor
Enough liquor to forget what it cost
My guitar became tune immune

Heartache became my friend
Staring at the bottom of another bottle
I'm living in a land of pretend
My guitar no longer remembers me

POSTCARDS IN THE MAIL

I've been sending postcards
Near and afar
Pending where you are
You sent the first one
When I visited home
Or at least it was the place I came from
It was from Coney Island of the Steeplechase
That's where we spent one of our last days
Walking around the lower New York Bay
You moved from the City
Back up north to Schenectady
Sure our time was brief

In Juneau I put a postcard in the mail
Had on it this photo of a whale
There wasn't many postcards for sale
But I'd just been to the Shrine of St Thérèse
Looked out on the water and saw three
Three whales staring back at me
So I wrote it on a postcard and sent it on its way
Hopefully it found you one day
It was a little wet from the rain
But the ink didn't run too much
I miss your voice
Your smell
Your smile
Your taste

And your touch
I got the postcards you sent
From your trip to Canada
Down to South America
And your brief stay in Chicago
I got your postcard from
Texas
Ohio
And Indiana
Atlanta
Nashville
And Louisville

I was up in Colorado
I trekked through the snow
To go to the nearest store
Had a postcard with a mountain on
They sure looked Rocky so I bought that one
One stamp and I'm done
The rest is up to the mail
Fort Collins town out of a fairytale
Odell Brewing
The Lincoln Center
Hattie McDaniel

I've been sending postcards man
Sent one from Paris
Spain
And Milan

Las Vegas
Missouri
And Oregon
Hope my message found you
Sure emails
Texts
And other such things would do
And they're probably more reliable too
But there's something that makes my heart skip a beat
Every time I see
I have a postcard from you waiting for me
What I guess I'm trying to say
Is maybe one day
When we are old and gray
I still hope we're making it places
To be putting postcards in the mail

I DON'T WANT TO DIE LIKE STEVE MCQUEEN

I don't want to die like Steve McQueen
In a clinic with a hidden identity
Wanting to live
Trying everything
I want to die like Hemingway
Choosing the final day
Living till his health had deteriorated
But long enough he'd waited
I don't want to die like Steve McQueen
Holding on harder than the doctors could believe
I want to live like Steve McQueen
Fast cars and fading memories
The King of Cool
And nobody's fool
I want to die like Hunter S. Thompson
Go when I decide to be done
Sure he too was a fighter
But the time came for him to rest upon his typewriter
I don't want to die like Andy Kaufman
Desperately trying to hold on
I don't want to die like Andy Warhol
On a hospital bed that's too small
I want to live like Steve McQueen
Fast
Loose
and a little mean
I want to live like Hunter S. Thompson

Fast
Loose
And completely free

THERAPISTS & MARGARITAS

I went to see a therapist
She told me I seemed stressed
I said "no shit"
She said I might be depressed
I thought to myself
This is really good for my self-esteem
Then I was told
To think back to being three years old
I told her that was a long time ago
My memory ain't so good
She asked if I drank
I asked for a whiskey please
She said that's not what she meant
Apparently
They don't serve drinks in therapy
So she said her best guess
Was to assume my answer was yes
Asked if I drank every day
I said only on special occasions
And in stressful situations
But otherwise I don't touch the stuff
It felt like she was trying to call my bluff
As my words she didn't seem to trust
Asked me if I was telling the truth
Because when she asked if I drank
I didn't need to think
Before asking for whiskey

I asked if this was a test
Because she already said I was stressed
It was like she didn't listen
This may not be a special occasion
But it was clearly a stressful situation
So we started again
Talked about my friends
Past girlfriends
And my parents
She then asked me
If I smoked weed
I thought finally
Told her I had a joint already rolled
But I'd also smoke a bowl
Turns out that was also not what she meant
She really needed to rephrase her questions
Then she told me to knock the dope on the head
Handed me a prescription for Spravato
I threw it away and caught happy hour at El Dorado
Margaritas
Tacos
The therapist
Tried her best
But I managed to relieve my own stress

THE STORY OF THE BED BUG BLUES

It was our first apartment
Koreatown
Opposite the Big 6 Market
Wooden floors in the kitchen
The other room had carpet
A bed near the window
A couch against the wall
A coffee table
A record player
And that was about all
So me and my buddy
Drove into the valley
La Crescenta
That drive can be horrific
The 101
And the LA traffic
We were picking up a cabinet
Because my lady had to have it
So we took my friend's pick-up truck
Collected the cabinet
Put the cabinet in the back
But in the back
I noticed a lack
Of anything to strap
The cabinet
To the back
So we backtracked
Put the cabinet back

And drove to the store
All because my buddy forgot the bungee cords
It was one of those dollar spots
The kind that sell the lot
But apparently not
Bungee cords
So we bought some twine
But they only had the real thin kind
I mean we could tear it with our hands
No scissors or knife required
We drove back
Picked the cabinet up
Tied her down
With all the twine around
We used the whole bunch
Still we worried it wasn't enough
But figured we'd try our luck
Man that twine really sucked
As soon as we hit the highway
The cabinet flew off the back of the truck
All the kings and queens in the world
They could bring all their horses
All their men
And their women
That cabinet could not be put together again
We drove back to my place
He didn't want to stay
He didn't want to see the look on her face
She took it pretty well

I mean my eye started to swell
But you couldn't really tell
Everything was okay
Nothing was ruining our moving in day
We were in love
She'd been unloading her car
Unpacking
Turning the place into a home
But when I was gone
She'd walked down to the parking lot
It was on her way back up
That she dropped
The new TV we bought
She showed me it still worked
Just occasionally the picture blurred
And there was a slight hole in the corner of the screen
I took it pretty well
Well I gave her a little hell
Then my other eye started to swell
I'm just kidding
Everything was okay
Nothing was ruining our moving in day
Some time went by
We'd been on the road
Going to whichever place we'd go
We'd been back a few days
She started scratching in many ways
The bed bug blues
They come to you

In the middle of the night
With their fucking bites
There's not much left to do
When you've got the bed bug blues
The mattress had to go
Everything had to be washed
Cleaned inside out
Ran every item of clothing through the dryer
I smoked
Toked
Choked and got a little higher
She told me it was not the time for marijuana
I said it might help to calm her
I should not have said that
After that
We cleaned in silence
A bed bug may be small but they can cause a lot of stress
Put our love to the test
They're relentless
So we went out and bought an air mattress
We got a high sized double
It was pretty comfy
And well during a certain activity
The air mattress lost its air
And we collapsed in on ourselves
Life was taking its toll
The TV finally broke
After a year of ignoring the hole
There was wear and tear

It was everywhere
We kept buying air mattresses
Because bed bugs don't like plastic
They prefer wood
Paper
And fabric
Soon our debates
Turned to arguments
Then the arguments turned to quiet
I'd found a puncture again
But I put some tape across it
Filled it with air
The fix was never meant
To be permanent
We'd started sleeping on our own sides
But in the middle of the night we were sure to collide
When the air mattress deflated
With our body weight
Everything was okay
Nothing ruined moving out day
She went to her mom's to stay
It had been a while
Since either of us smiled
So I wrote the saddest of songs
And went a rambling on
But the song was so sad
I locked it in a box
I played it once
I called it *The Bed Bug Blues*

CALIFORNIA GRIZZLY BEAR

I'm a goddamn California grizzly bear
I'm the picture on the flag up there
The ornament on your window ledge
I inspired the shape of that topiary hedge
I'm the tattoo on that person's arm
I'm the stormy waters and the calm
The mascot for your university
And I'm on the jerseys of their football teams
But I've been extinct going on a century
I suppose accounts of me are legendary
Although I heard they were talking about reintroducing me
In this California territory
I'm a goddamn California grizzly

SMELL OF CIGARETTES & SEX

I smell of cigarettes
I smell of sex
I smell of whiskey
And I smell of regrets

I sound like bullshit
I sound of nothing
I sound like my own words
Sound less remembered and more forgotten

I smell of hiding
I smell of lying
I smell of weed
And I smell like trying

I sound lost
I sound like I paid some cost
I sound like I'm flying
And I'm starting to sound like I'm dying

I smell of cigarettes
I smell like sex
I smell of ol' whiskey
And I smell of regrets

CHANGING SEASONS

Changing seasons
Altering feelings
Altering seasons
And
Changing feelings

The heat of the summer
Is going straight to my head
Too warm on my couch
Too hot in my bed
No air conditioning
The fan on my ceiling
Only blows dust around
And I can't bear the sound
Sure the heat gets to me
But I do like to feel
The summer days
Down by the beach
Barbecues
Salads and finger foods
White wine
And cocktails
Shake me up
One of Jimmy Buffet's
Hurricanes
Take me away
It's another summer day

Leaves on the ground
Autumn is around
There's a bite in the air
The wind doesn't seem to care
That I'm trying to light
A cigarette
In the middle of this autumnal night
The rain begins to fall
I'm trying to keep dry
Clinging to an already forgotten summertime
Ignoring the signs
That winter is approaching
But tonight
I'm enjoying this October night
Pumpkin pie
And apple spice
Cinnamon
And candle lights
Orange and brown
Fall's around

The winter has set in
Heavy rain
And fading light
Can be a little depressing
But sometimes funerals are easier than weddings
The falling snow
The Christmas show
And tales of long ago

Marinate through us all
We move to winter from the fall
My hands are cold
I can't feel my feet
My ass is starting to freeze
Sitting on this empty bus stop seat
But I'm not getting thinner
Hearty meals
And turkey dinners
Mashed potato and gravy
Hot chocolates
And whiskey
Overcoats
And frozen roads
How winter tends to come and go

The seasons keep changing
Time eventually brings
The hopeful spring
Longer days start to set in
I always liked the darker nights my friend
But every day eventually must come to an end
The joys of spring
The Ides of March
Everything seems to end before it starts
Labor Day
Cinco de Mayo the fifth of May

Hunting eggs
People pretending to observe lent
Chocolate bunnies
And Jesus freaks
Marshmallow peeps
And sugary treats
It's the time
For April showers
And sacramental wine
Summer
Fall
Winter
And spring
I suppose every season
Has a beginning and an end

Changing feelings
Altering seasons
Altering feelings
And
Changing seasons

THE BALLAD OF JOHN TANNER

There was a boy
By the name of John
But everyone
Called him Jack
He was a dreamer
And he truly believed
He had what it takes
To head to LA
And make his big break
Into the homes of families
Acting out stories
On their TV screens
So he moved out west
And to be an actor he went
Had a beat up old car
And a few months' rent
Young Jack Tanner
Once sang *The Star-Spangled Banner*
To his entire class
In his home state of Arkansas
They all would applaud
And gave him a standing ovation
And the motivation
To pursue all of his dreams
He was young
Good looking
And sweet

A big Hollywood agent he was hoping to meet
So he drove to the office
Of William Morris
Said he may be the greatest actor there has ever been
Only problem
Was it was still waiting to be seen
He didn't have an acting reel
I mean
He once played Joseph in the school nativity
An agent happened to be walking on by
Jack Tanner was immediately signed
He was going to finally
Make his way to the TV
Or silver screen
I'm just kidding
He was thrown out by security
His name wasn't known
So they sent him on home
Money started getting low
There wasn't even a sniff of a television show
He'd always heard
Most actors are servers first
So he applied to wait tables
He needed a job more stable
Servers get tips
Minimum wage is shit
So he went off to some restaurants
And a few bars
But he didn't get very far

He was having no luck
Applied to work at Starbucks
Had an interview
Went pretty well
At least until
They told him one day to try again
Tried three times before they finally hired him
He was serving a guy
Who told Jack the limit was the sky
Gave Jack his card
Told him he had an office on Wilshire Boulevard
So Jackie gave him a call
Turns out the guy wasn't in show business at all
The man instead asked Jack to strip
Jack was about to split
Then he asked how much
How much it would be to strip but not be touched
Guy said a hundred bucks
But he'd give five hundred if he was willing to suck
You get the picture
Jack left a hundred bucks richer
All he had to do was stand and wait
While this older dude would masturbate
Sure it wasn't the gig he wanted
But he said to me
It always beat the shit out of serving coffee
Said the customers were so rude
He preferred standing in the nude
Every week

Tuesday afternoon
Then Tuesdays and Thursdays
Sometimes Fridays
He'd head to Wilshire Boulevard
Before he started to know it
He was making five hundred to blow it
He wanted to call home
But he didn't want his family to know
So he didn't tell anyone
Left Starbucks as time passed
He started tripling his money in exchange for his ass
But now he could afford an acting class
Bought himself headshots
The lot
He prepared a scene
From *Frankie and Johnny*
In the Clair de Lune
It was safe to assume
He couldn't have fallen harder
For his scene partner
He'd never loved anyone like he fell in love with her
She really seemed to care
They kissed one night under the setting sun
He was scared that she was sure to run
If he told her of the work he'd done
So he told the guy
He'd no longer be coming by
Offered Jackie more money
But he refused

The man said Jackie was free to choose
So back to Starbucks he went
Absolutely hell bent
On achieving his goal
Of landing a TV role
But him and this girl had grown really close
Everyone commented that they seemed closer than most
Imagining children and wedding toasts
But secrets tend to grow
And she landed a role on a TV episode
Her career started to take hold
He was left standing in the cold
Before too long
Most of his money was gone
She was going to parties
In Hollywood homes with celebrities
He was thinking of old memories
And his time on his knees
He just wanted to be free
And be the one
Making money
On TV
But he kept punching the clock
At his day job
Brewing coffee pots
In a coffee shop
He saw her less and less
With her growing success
Worrying about the secrets he kept

He got a new scene partner
Because her career kept going farther
Eventually she'd walk away not to be seen by him again
Well he'd see her again
But not in person
Saw her on a movie screen
Saw her on his TV
Saw her in tabloids
Rumored to be dating celebrities
He was walking home
Down Santa Monica Boulevard
In front of him stopped a car
He recognized the man
Who asked if everything was going according to plan
A few years had passed
Since they saw each other last
With a tear in his eye
Resisting the urge to cry
Jackie asked the guy to drive
Said he hadn't been feeling alive
He wanted to scream and shout
The city was eating him up and spitting him out
Said he was back at Starbucks
Down on his luck
They didn't go to his office
They drove to a bar
They drank all night long
Jackie wondered where it all went wrong
After a few drinks

He started to think
Think about young Jackie Tanner
Singing *The Star-Spangled Banner*
He thought of his dreams
And their fading reality
His lost future wife
His failed acting life
Jack asked the man
If his body was still in demand
He was desperate for cash
And believed love doesn't last
But to Jackie's surprise
The man declined
Said his ex-wife left him without a dime
And he never paid to fuck
He paid because with Jack he was in love
Said he'd never paid for sex before
Had never picked up any whores
He hadn't done it before
And hasn't done it since
He was hoping for romance
So he took his chance
But he learned affection isn't something you can buy
He just had to try
He'd never been in love with a guy
Just to be clear
Jackie had no idea
This was his first time hearing
The man's true feelings

The room fell quiet
All you could hear was breathing
Till Jackie said he'd stopped believing
In everything
Hollywood
Picket fences
And diamond rings
The Lakers were on the TV
In the commercials they did see
An advertisement for a new movie
Jackie's ex Hannah was the lead
Her career was flying
But inside she was dying
She truly loved John Tanner
I know she left
Wrapped up in her movie star promise
But if she was being honest
She was completely lost
She wasn't the only one to blame
Jack was struggling to handle her fame
Nothing stayed the same

It was a warm summer night
Hottest day of the year
At home stayed Jack Tanner
Safest place during the winds of Santa Ana
The Hollywood starlet was stumbling home
From the bar at the Chateau Marmont
The older gentlemen was driving down Sunset

Too drunk for any regrets
He recognized the starlet walking
He stopped the car and got to talking
About young John Tanner
To his old flame Hannah
He offered her a ride
She initially said she was fine
But after some conversation
She gave in to his persuasion
He drove Hannah to her new Hollywood home
The two of them were both alone
The morning eventually came
The maid let herself in
That's when she saw both of them
A passionate crime
She'd been stabbed multiple times
Laying lifeless on the living room floor
Blood on the carpets and blood on the door
She clearly tried to crawl
After she slid down the wall
Phone off the hook like she was trying to make a call
After she drew her last breath
And he was sure she was dead
He put a bullet through his own head
Jack saw the news
He didn't know what to do
He was confused
Hannah had no family
So she left all of her money

To young John Tanner
Said it was the least she could do
For what she'd put him through
But he'd always wonder if she ever knew
If before he killed her
Did he tell her the truth?
Her life would end
Because of an old friend
I mean they'd have never met
If Jackie didn't let
The man give him cash
To fund his acting class
Sure she was young
But she'd planned for her death
Considering she had no family left
The funeral was televised
The public mourned
The public cried
Jack was dead inside
But she always loved his voice
So despite the pain it would bring
He accepted her request to sing
So John Tanner
Sang *The Star-Spangled Banner*
Live on the TV
For the whole world to see
It was the only time
You will ever find
Jack Tanner on a TV screen

His family tuned in
And they finally got to see
The young man on TV
After the funeral Jack went straight home
He was completely alone
No hope
Only a hanging rope
He kicked out the chair
Wanting it to end there
But the rope did snap
So on the floor he sat
Drinking whiskey and sleeping pills
Until
He finally fell still
It all came to an end
Jackie would never breathe again
The phone it rang
But there was no-one to answer
It went to the machine
Some record label guy had seen
John Tanner
Singing *The Star-Spangled Banner*
He wanted to make a deal
To record an LP
But Jackie's voice will only ever be
A long lost memory
Sure he was seen on TV
But it was a show he never wanted to see

INK ON PAPER

My words are nothing
Ink on paper
Sure I put them in order
Tried to let them make sense
Sometimes they seem sad
Sometimes they seem *rad*
And often the word choice is bad
Like choosing to write the word *rad*
I'm not judging the expression
I'm just saying the use of the word
Should be brought into question
Before
The ink hits the page
I mean the word *rad* could create
An academic rage
But I'll tell them to just turn the page
Not to worry
Just relax
It's only ink on paper
Sure there are intentions
And some ideas I mention
But don't take everything so seriously
I only put some words together how I want them to be
Sure some ideas
Are deeper
Than others
But it doesn't matter

Read what you want
Believe what you want
I'll write what I want
I'll see what I want to see
Because I'm exactly who I want to be
You can either take or leave

COCAINE

Let's buy another drink
It's getting too late to think
My feet are starting to sink
But my brain is awake
Awake is my brain
Cocaine

Let's smoke a cigarette
Our troubles we can forget
Let's do it again to ease any regret
Insane is how I feel
I feel insane
Cocaine

Let's get out of here
Pick up a pack of beers
I can see so clear
My veins are tingling
Blood tingling in my veins
Cocaine

Let's go back to mine
Party for the rest of time
I want to become one with your mind
The rain is falling
The falling rain
Cocaine

Let's get ourselves dry
Then we can try
To get a little extra high
The pain is eased by your kiss
Kisses ease the pain
Cocaine

POGO THE CLOWN

Some childhoods are hard
Others never get a chance to start
Mine ripped out my heart
Took me through hell in a handcart

I was raised with fear
My daddy lived on whiskey and beer
He was never shy to make his opinions clear
Said I was a sissy then he called me a queer

Beat me till I thought I'd die
Leather straps and broomsticks
Whatever was near by
I was knocked unconscious but I still wanted to try
To buy his love so I learned not to cry

All my younger days I was tested
They were supposed to be a family friend
I wasn't supposed to be molested
I kept quiet I was too scared I'd be detested
They certainly detested me when I was arrested

They had a pretty heavy case
I couldn't hide behind my painted face
Even if the bodies in the river were never to surface
They just found 27 bodies in my crawl space

The corpses of young boys and young men were found
My house in Norwood Park is where I kept them bound
They're getting the injection ready to put me down
So come on down to Statesville Correctional Facility and
Say goodbye to Pogo the Clown

EVERYONE WANTS TO KILL

I was helping old Marge close down the bar
I was stacking chairs she was counting the till
A couple of guys burst in
Demanded a refill
Told them we weren't open still
But they said they wouldn't leave until
They'd had their glasses filled
Marge cocked back her shotgun and threatened to fill
Fill them with buckshot
And promised the second shot would kill
And kill
Then kill again
They left
The audience cheered
A few liberals jeered
But the story ain't over
It was late October
A few evenings later
They stormed in like a tornado
This time not just the two
But they brought along a whole crew
Took every cent in the entire place
Then one mean bastard punched old Marge in the face
Said if she called the cops
This wouldn't stop
Then they left
After the theft

Screaming if she called the police
They would come back and kill
Kill everyone
Then keep killing
I suppose the audience is still watching
I mean the third act always tends to have the most action
After all
Ain't that the attraction?
Well
Marge wasn't one to be fucked with
She iced her eye and smoked a spliff
Called her boys on the phone
Told them to bring their friends along
Said there was some hunting to do
They came right over with a bunch of other guys too
Of course I was also there
To leave at that moment didn't seem fair
So we each grabbed our guns
And into the night we would run
See Marge knew where those guys came from
She knew everyone that came along
We came up on this house
All of a sudden gunfire breaks out
Marge's youngest is shot off his feet
The audience is on the edge of their seats
Watching with nothing but thrills
As the boys asking for refills
Get killed
Marge gets killed

Marge's sons get killed
I get killed
Shit
We all got killed
I was laying there
Taking my final breaths
Heard the TV playing
Newsman was saying
So many people had been shot dead
I thought the news couldn't be that quick to spread
It wasn't
He was talking about a shooting in a different town
So many damned shootings around
Then the breaking news came on
There's a high speed chase with OJ Simpson
I can't help but tune in
Can't move anyway
The amount of blood I'm losing
I'm the audience and I'm clutching my chest
Letting the Bronco do the rest
With my final breaths
I suppose people like to see killing
Watch people kill
Hear people kill
How many people need to be killed?
For everyone to be fulfilled

THE OLD, WHITE, REPUBLICAN RIGHT, TIGHT FISTED, SHORT SIGHTED, SAVING THE RICH TONIGHT BLUES

I'm in the top one percent
I could give my money away
But I'd prefer it
If you were to pay me rent
I mean
How am I supposed to pay these taxes to the government?
I vote red in the US
And blue in the UK
I say
We ban weddings for gays
It's what the word of God says
I'm a Christian too
Believe in the Bible through and through
I particularly like the part
When Jesus gives the people his assurance
That he won't heal the sick unless they have insurance
I'm old and white
Abortion clinics just aren't right
These women need to pray
Because surely that's a man's right to say
I mean I have five kids
So I must be an authority
Sure I'm divorced and none of my kids talk to me
They say I should donate
My worth and my estate
All to charity

But I made the check payable to me
I think I might have to buy my way into heaven
I only ever thought about myself
And ways to increase my wealth
There's a priest at my funeral
And nobody else
Casket made of gold
As I lay all alone
Money can't get me out of this hole
I may be surrounded by gold but I'm covered in dirt
I spent my life trying to buy bottled water in the desert
I've got *the old, white, republican right, tight fisted, short sighted, saving the rich tonight blues*

'FORE I'M DEAD

There's some books on my shelf
That I haven't read
Stories that were written
That I may not read 'fore I'm dead

There's music on an LP
I haven't heard yet
Melodies and lyrics created
That I may not hear 'fore I'm dead

There's food I haven't tasted
Certain foods I've never been fed
Like foie gras and caviar
May never taste goose liver 'fore I'm dead

There's whiskey in a barrel I haven't sipped
Whiskey I haven't drunk to regret
Like the Sinatra Select
I may never try it 'fore I'm dead

There's words left on my tongue
Words I haven't said
May not get the chance
To say those words 'fore I'm dead

THE CIGARETTE STOOP

I may not be breaking news with this disclaimer
And disclaimers are not something I like to write
But I like to tell people
In case they fell through the cracks
Smoking cigarettes isn't good for you
It's just something I like to do
It makes you short of breath
Coughing up half your chest
And your mouth does not feel fresh
But I'd be telling tales
If I told you
I didn't enjoy
Every inhale
The reason I'm sharing this
Is because only smokers might know this
When you're a smoker you tend to make friends
Even if it is just for a few minutes
While we're now forced to stand outside
Smokers tend to congregate
While the non-smokers wait
I was living in this place
An apartment complex
Los Angeles
Had a stoop out front
That's where I'd sit
To smoke my cigarettes
Sometimes it would be quiet

Sometimes people would stop and talk to me
I'd sit out there with a coffee
Or maybe some tea
And
Occasionally
I've been known to sip on some whiskey

I was on that very stoop
When I saw a taxi pull up
Took a sip from my coffee cup
As I heard the door behind me unlock
And out walked the most beautiful girl
I had never laid eyes on such beauty before
I mean my goddamn jaw dropped to the floor
She smiled
I picked my jaw up
Smiled back
She got in the taxi
I stayed on the stoop
Had another smoke
While I thought
I'd never seen that girl before
I wondered if she lived here
Or was visiting someone she knows
But then I thought
At least she may visit again
Because she must at least have a friend
To be in the building
But then I thought

She may be visiting a boyfriend
I suppose all good things come to an end
Like my cigarette
So I went back inside

A few hours later
There I was
Back out front
Ol' Larry was talking to me
He doesn't hear so good
And he mumbles when he speaks
He was mumbling as he spoke to me
But from what I understood
His rent payment had to be delayed
He was waiting for a check to be paid
As usual the government was late
I was in between smokes
The building manager walked by
So Larry went to talk to the guy
Then ol' Maggie came out
Smoking her Marlboro Golds
Not the regular ones
The 100's
She asked if I was okay
I just said yeah because what else are you supposed to say?
Told me she was going back east
Just for a few weeks
Thanksgiving
She'd stay with her family

Her son and his wife
Their two children
Three and five
The oldest a boy
The youngest a girl
Maggie lives alone
Her husband was a veteran
I never met him
They met in their teens
She always said
He was never the same
But who goes to war and doesn't change?

I sat out there the next few weeks
But I didn't see
The girl
You know
The girl that got in the taxi
The girl of my dreams
The janitor sees me
And asks me for a smoke
I tell him it's not a problem
He looks ready to take off his load
Sit down a minute
Relax a minute
And smoke
He'd known me a while
Told me a new weed shop had opened
About eight blocks away

And the deals were supposed to be okay
Told him I'd check it out one day
But I was still buying dope the old fashioned way
He had to get back to work
I had to move on with my day

Sometime after midnight
I sat with my bourbon
While I watched a couple fight
They were really screaming at each other
She was shouting something about him being a loser
And he seemed pretty adamant that he was not a loser
They reached a stalemate
He left
Walked away
She sat down on the opposite side of the stoop
Lit a cigarette
She was fighting back the tears
I asked if she was okay
She told me to go fuck myself
And also walked away
But in a different direction
You meet all kinds of people when you're smoking
The landlord was coming out of the front door
Said I couldn't smoke there anymore
I said "I know you told me before"
I was supposed to be ten feet from the entrance
So I got up
Moved off the stoop

And stood on the sidewalk
Him and I continued to talk
Something about basketball
I waited for him to go back inside
Before I went back to the stoop
Sat myself down
Looked around
Lit up again
Exactly when
My neighbor's boyfriend
Showed up and I let him in
Let him in the building
It was at that moment I really hoped
They hadn't broken up
But they hadn't
She was happy to see him
They were in love
The kind of love
That's contagious
Like it kinda makes you want it
Do you know the kind?
I suppose it's rare to find

It was about seven at night
I'd just gotten home from work
Took up my seat on the stoop
Ready for a cigarette
My thoughts I needed to collect
I was tired

I hadn't eaten and the night before wasn't much for sleeping
I saw the landlord through the window
When I walked past
So I knew I was safe to sit
Without him giving a shit
Ol' Larry was coming on home
Told me things were pretty good
He just received a check
Which he didn't expect
Said he's putting it towards next month's rent
Ol' Maggie opened the door
Larry went on his way
They never got along
But that's a story for another day
Ol' Maggie
Started telling me about her vacation
Showed me pictures on her phone
I looked at them
Didn't want to be rude
Even though I was in need of food
And a little peace
It was too many people to see
As the janitor clocked out
Ready to leave
He said goodnight to Maggie
And shook hands with me
Maggie was tired and went to retire
Told me she'd see me tomorrow

That's when I saw
The guy and the girl
From the other night
When they were arguing
About whether he was
Or was not
A loser
Well that night they were holding hands
Walked in together to the building next to mine
Then my neighbor came out with her boyfriend
I wondered when it would all end
I was hungry
My fridge was empty
I was lonesome
But tired of people on my stoop
But my neighbor looked so happy
And so did he
Date night
Exciting
A taxi pulled up
And I could not believe my luck
There she was
Standing in front of me
The most beautiful girl
To step foot in this world
She'd finally come back
I was prepared
I thought about that moment so many times
I smiled

She smiled
I said "hi"
She said "hi"
I said "you live here?"
She said "yes"
I said "cool"
She said "Have you eaten?"
I said "yes"
She said "okay"
I've never seen her again

ISIS

I'm thinking about *Isis*
Isis inspired me
That statement can seem
Like it may cause controversy
But I don't want you to get me wrong
I'm talking about the Bob Dylan song
Where he was married in May but it didn't last long
I'm talking about *Isis*
Not radical beliefs or confused ideology
Not blood shed nor eternal fire
I'm talking about a Dylan song from the album *Desire*
1976
Isis
Abu Bakr al-Baghdadi
Never sang a *Mozambique* or a *One More Cup of Coffee*
He may have had fear in his name
But he was never capable of writing *Hurricane*
So when you talk about Isis
I'll acknowledge they're the villain
But every time you say Isis to me I will
Start singing the song by Bob Dylan

RATTLE-SNAKES FOR FELONS

Britain had a law
A long long time ago
I'm talking early 1700s
The law was written
That the convicts of Britain
Could be transported
Across Atlantic waters
So in 1751
Ben Franklin thought he'd have some fun
Published a satire in the Pennsylvania Gazette
Said they should wait until spring and then collect
The rattlesnakes as they come out of their holes
While they're feeble and slow
Then he'd send some on a boat
And off to England they should go
To be distributed across all of the land
From St James's Park to the Prime Minister's garden
Britain said they sent the felons to help America populate
Franklin didn't want a favor he wanted a trade
Rattle-Snakes for Felons
Three years later he published about rattlers again
A cartoon of a snake cut into segments
Join or Die it was a call to unite
In order to win the fight
French and Indian war
A hope to be divided no more
Some people used to believe

If a cut-up snake was put together again before sunset
It would begin to breathe
Brought back to life
I don't think it's true
But Franklin liked to talk about rattlesnakes
Seemed to respect them make no mistake
Said they always need a reason to attack
But when they do there's no looking back
Another thing he liked
They always send a warning before they strike
Join or die
Was the cry
Some kind of idea that we are stronger as one
United
Not cut up and divided
18th century
To the 21st century
Division is all I seem to see

BROKE

I missed a call from the bank
They were trying to tell me
My phone bill was unable to be paid
Insufficient funds
I figured
My phone had been cut off

Broke
Oh so broke

My landlord knocked on the door
So I stayed as quiet as I could
He slipped a note under my door
'twas a notice
I figured
My rent was late and not by just a few days

Broke
Oh so broke

A letter in my mailbox
Said I owed money to the LADWP
The bar I was working in closed
I was in between paychecks
So I figured
This might be the case

Broke
Oh so broke

I've been broke before
Probably be broke again
And it's likely I'll be broke in between
But my friends will always be
Better than yours
I'm not trying to be rude
I'm saying that because
Anyone that tries to be a friend to me
Isn't worried about any of my money
They know I'm broke

Broke
Oh so broke

REDLINE PART 1

I was on the redline
The redline runs from downtown
To North Hollywood
It is an underground train
On the maps the line is red
Hence the name
I rode that line most days
I was heading from the station at MacArthur Park
It was a little after dark
I was going to Hollywood and Vine
A frequent stop of mine
But around Wilshire and Beverly we stopped
We waited to see if it would start again
A man started talking to me
His jeans were torn
His sneakers were worn
Asked me what I did
I told him I was a rambling kid
He said he was a talent agent
Told me to take his card
I thought it was bullshit
But I took his card
Didn't want to be rude
I wasn't trying to judge the dude
I got to work a little early
So I ordered some food
And I sat watching the news

Then I saw a picture of the guy
The guy from the redline
He was wanted
By the police
Murder in the first degree
You meet all kinds of people on the redline

I WISH I COULD MEET YOU FOR THE FIRST TIME AGAIN

I wish I could meet you for the first time again
If only I could have known then
What I've learned since
Maybe everything would be different
Perhaps it would be the same
I suppose it could be worse
And we might just be cursed
I'd at least try first

I wouldn't try to make you fall in love
I'd just want to be in your life enough
To celebrate your victories
And pick you up when times get rough
I'd walk you home from every bar
Let you turn me into the airbag in your car
Make myself the lid of your jar

If I was able to hit rewind
And take the both of us back in time
To when we first met
I hope you'd still be a friend of mine
But your lips I'd try not to kiss
What I never had is harder to miss
But I suppose I never minded staring out into the abyss

IT'S COLD ON THIS BARROOM FLOOR

It's dark in this old barroom
It's cold on the floor
Nowhere I haven't laid before
I only ever managed to keep my mouth shut
When I wasn't supposed to
Like not telling you I loved you
Or even saying I loved you too
But here I am in a barroom
Being punched off my stool
Because I've always been quick to say fuck you
And even quicker to say fuck you too
Well this guy
He took me by surprise
Gave me a mean right hook before I realized
There was even a fight taking place
Sucker punched
And I don't know why
Well I suppose
I may have some idea
I mean
I didn't know she was his lady
When I asked her to dance
I was just taking a chance
She said yes
That is a fact
So I'm sorry if he was mad about that
Maybe he was mad she kissed me back

I don't know
I guess there's a few reasons he may have had
Bartender
Please
Pour me one more
It's cold down here on this barroom floor

LIMERENCE or MUSE

I saw a meteor flash through the sky
I was hoping it came crashing to earth on top of you and I
Because I already feel like I've been swallowed up whole
And if I haven't then I'm only selling my soul
I don't know which is more tiring
Being loved too much
Or not loved enough

You were the deadliest drug with the most dangerous high
But like all drugs the high becomes harder to come by
Eventually that kind of living takes its toll
But I'm bored of everyone else seeming in control
Sure the rain put the flames out but the sparks are still firing
And I'm lost in your touch
I'm just sorry my heart had to grow so tough

THE CECIL HOTEL

Opened in 1927
A cheap place to stay
In the heart of downtown LA
But to those that knew it well
Knew it was the gates of hell
Right there on Main Street
At the Cecil Hotel

First recorded suicide was in 1931
A resident
Ingested poison
Then a year on
A maid found a young man
He'd also kicked the can
After the trigger was pulled
Ruled a suicide
No note but it's not like anyone lies
Next few years more people died
Poison drinking
Throat slashing
Window falling
And window jumping
Wasn't really *the place to go*
A 19 year old
Threw her newborn
Out of the window

Blood dripping in the paint
Leaking through the floors
Blood on all the windows
And all over the doors
There was a report
That somebody saw
None other than Elizabeth Short
At Cecil's bar
She was apparently staying not too far
At a place called The Biltmore
So she could have been to Cecil's before
No way to know
It's not all we may ever know
Like where the Black Dahlia's killer would go?

The Cecil Hotel
640 S. Main Street
Where Richard Ramirez used to sleep
During part of his killing spree
Hand guns
Tire irons
And machetes
Anything to inflict his savagery
Apparently
He was a Satanist
And he died on death row
But some say his ghost
Still roams
The corridors of the suicide hotel

Because the Night Stalker was too evil to make it into hell
So in the hotel
By the gates he dwells
Or that's the story they tell
I suppose murder sells

Jack Unterweger stayed at the Cecil
In 1991
Even went on a police ride along
Sure he'd murdered someone
Back in 1974
But he was released on parole
The year before
His trip to LA
After his successful attempt to rehabilitate
He came to LA to investigate
The red-light district of the city
So police showed him where to be
Good ol' helpful LAPD
Then he killed three women
Killed more in
Czechoslovakia
And in
Austria

In 2013
Came the story you wouldn't believe
Poor Elisa Lam
Born in 1991

British Colombia
She was a student
About to head north to Santa Cruz
Something she wouldn't get to do
Actually
She wouldn't be seen alive again
Missing
Completely vanished
Almost a month later
A number of guests at the hotel
Claimed the water wasn't running well
Some said the water was black
Some said the water had a smell
They went to the rooftop
And all their hearts sank
When they opened the water tank
They found
Naked and drowned
The body of Elisa Lam
Ruled a suicide
But I don't know
She looked scared in that elevator video
Some say she climbed in
Some say she was forced in
Some say it was the work of Satan
But that's all speculation
If you're thinking about a vacation
Maybe in LA
Don't worry about The Cecil Hotel's dark fame

They guarantee you it's not the same
After all they changed their name
The Cecil Hotel is now called the Stay on Main

I WANT A GIRL WITH HEROIN EYES

I want a girl with those heroin eyes
The kind of eyes that confides
You might think they're lying
But the truth is no surprise

I want a girl that makes me wake up
And I don't mean just a fuck
I mean the kind of girl
The kind of girl where you can't believe your luck

I want a girl that's set on thinking
Which usually entails an amount of drinking
If you think hard enough you too will understand
Alcohol can help you drown but the bottle keeps you from sinking

I want a girl that shoots whiskey
Drinks pints and acts free
Lives for today
That's the perfect girl for me

I want a girl that makes me want to be a better man
The best man I can
Only problem is I'm not too stable
So she would really need to understand

I want a girl with heroin eyes
Let's just both get high
While we're too young
Too young to realize

A SHAKESPEAREAN SONNET

I'm writing a sonnet like Bill Shakespeare
He sure seemed to abide by a few rules
I think I need to crack open a beer
And just try to write something that sounds cool

Paul Newman in *Cool Hand Luke* that will do
Because I can Steve McQueen in *Bullitt*
Was Richard Burton cool taming the shrew?
Something not cool is Billy Ray's mullet

I have nothing against mullets it rhymes
No offense to Cyrus I'd hate to break
His *achy breaky heart* it's seen hard times
Couldn't break it again for rhyming's sake

Ten syllables left beer straight to my head
Dreams of iambic pentameter dead

CALABASAS

They tell me I'm reckless
Tell me I'm careless
Well
I couldn't care less
I take care of my mess
With minimal stress
A little stress
No less
But life is full of tests
I know I ain't the best
And I'm amongst the rest
Sure I'm blessed
I'm breathing from my chest
But that's normal amongst the living I must confess
Shooting bullets at my bulletproof vest
For reasons beyond my greatest guess
Turning the meaningful into the meaningless
Killing time out here in old Calabasas

MARK 16:18

Jamie Coots was a Pentecostal pastor
True believer and snake handler
Father of Cody Coots
Maybe Jamie's arrest
Was just God's test
He was given probation
For the illegal transportation
Of five copperheads
Chattanooga
Eventually he got bit
And in keeping with the religion
Jamie and his family refused treatment
Because treatment was inconsistent
With their beliefs
It was the Full Gospel Tabernacle
During the ceremony
The Timber rattler sunk its teeth
Into Jamie Coots' right hand
He kept preaching as he died
In Middlesboro
Kentucky
He might be considered unlucky
Or perhaps he was a fool
Who am I to say?
That he might be alive today
If the paramedics hadn't been turned away
In exchange of medicine the family prayed

Which left his son Cody handling the snakes
Everything was great until he was bitten on the face
Disoriented and against his will
He was taken to the hospital
He survived
But if it was up to Cody he would have surely died
Up on a mountain top
One that God forgot
I suppose
Interpretation is more important than it seems
I mean
Read
Mark 16:18
People will believe anything

CHRISTMAS DAY IN LOS ANGELES

It's Christmas Day in Los Angeles
The streets are clearer than you'd ever see
It seems like everybody
Has traveled home
Everyone just visits this city y'know
Most
Only last a year or two
Before a life of dreaming falls through
Back up north
Back to the south
Across to the midwest
It doesn't matter where
Every Christmas
There's a mass exodus
And the cities left bare
With false snow
Decorated palm trees
Chinese food and Kentucky whiskey
It's Christmas Day in Los Angeles
I worked the bar Christmas Eve
Not many customers
But tips they would love to leave
As a little Christmas bonus for me
I suppose we paid for each others' company
Christmas Day in LA
People go to the movies
Maybe a diner

Meet up with their rag-tag friends
The ones with either no place to go
Or not enough money to travel home
It's Christmas Day in Los Angeles
Raise a glass of whatever you can find
Let's drink till the spirits ease our mind
Sure the sky is blue
And it might not be as cold as we're used to
But we do what we do
When it's Christmas Day in Los Angeles

THE DEVIL'S MUSIC

As the story goes
Robert Johnson made his way to the crossroads
To meet the Devil and hand him his soul
In exchange
He became the best blues player to be known
No chance of stepping into heaven
When he fell dead at twenty-seven
But God digs trumpets
Choirs
And harps
Not delta blues and rock stars
I was wondering which church was right
So
I listened to some people preach
But they all seemed the Billy Graham types
They didn't shine any light
To try and answer my plight
I did some reading
See if that gave me something to believe in
I read the Torah
The Quran
The Bible
And the Tao Te Ching
Answers they did not bring
Much like those that have gone before me
I got down on my knees
I didn't go down to the river

But oh boy did I pray
I had no idea what to say
I'd only just begun
And I began to hear Robert Johnson play
It was his guitar
There could be no mistake
The sound of Johnson
Can't be faked
Then all of a sudden
Some guy appeared
But I didn't feel a bit of fear
Guy seemed pretty friendly
Went by the name Max Yasgur
Said he owned a plot of land
In a far corner of hell
He was pretty quick to tell
Hell wasn't such a bad place to dwell
There's coffee
Whiskey
And a marijuana smell
I thought it sounded pretty good to me
So I asked what I needed to do
To make sure I made it through
The gates of hell
That's when Max said to me
"Son you just need to be free
Whether it be
A cassette
A record

A CD
Or an mp3
Turn that music up
To the notch that says don't give a fuck
And let the sweet Devil's blues
Wash on over you"
He then began
To tell me what he planned
Told me he bought the plot of land
To be like the farm he used to own
In a place called Bethel
New York state
1969
He was putting together a show
He was expecting everyone to go
Heard people in heaven
Have even started to sin
Thinking about what could have been
If they didn't live a life of pretend
Maybe they wouldn't be stuck in heaven
And they'd be able to attend
The greatest concert there's ever been
There's no Mormon Tabernacle Choir
There is Hendrix
Morrison
And Cobain
In hellfire
No headliners
Everyone plays as long as they want

Prince
Zappa
And George Harrison
Merle Haggard
BB King
And Duane Allman
What a show
I just had to know
Who else was going
Lynyrd Skynyrd is going to be fronted by Ronnie Van Zant
Lou Reed
Marc Bolan
And Townes Van Zandt
Joey
Johnny
Tommy
And Dee Dee Ramone
They are sure to perform
Marvin Gaye
Freddie Mercury
And Bob Marley
Stevie Ray Vaughn
Janis Joplin
And David Bowie
Oh wowie
Woody Guthrie met John Lennon
Johnny Cash apparently introduced them
They apparently formed a trio
Some experimental stuff

Heard Muddy Waters plays with them from time to time
When he's not recording with Bo Diddly and Sam Cooke
Occasionally Sinatra lends his voice
With Dean and Sammy and the good ol' boys
C'mon man
Let's be honest
All good music belongs to the Devil
Sorry if it offends
But I can't pretend
That Max Yasgur didn't answer my question
When he appeared that night
I'd spent my life
Trying to search
For religion
But music will always be my church
The kind of music played by
Ray Charles
Gram Parsons
And Nat King Cole
Daniel Johnston
Leadbelly
And Nico
The show could continue forever
There's even rumors Pac and Biggie might spit together
I asked Max if all this was true
He said "I'll show you"
And without further ado
On the drums appeared Keith Moon
He sneezed

And out of his nose flew
None other than Howlin' Wolf
Enough was enough
I didn't need any further proof
To know this was the truth
I just wanted to know the date
Max said I'd have to wait
Said the lineup wasn't complete
He was still waiting for some people to meet
But he told me not to worry
And not to be surprised
If all the good music seems to die
One day my dream will be realized
In the Devil's blues I'll be baptized
Robert Johnson
Sold his soul
So the world would know
How the blues should go
I asked Max if I could meet the Devil
Maybe I could go to the crossroads
Make a deal to sell my soul
Be the greatest writer the world has ever known
Well…
You may or may not be able to tell
My soul I wasn't able to sell
Devil was too busy tending to hell
Besides Robert Johnson always knew the blues pretty well

UNTITLED #10

Hide me in between your arms
Hold me in your endless charm
The wind is howling
But you're keeping me calm
Dogs are barking and I can hear car alarms
So much noise
Take me back to that ol' farm
This city living is becoming too hard

OH SWEET MISTY

Oh sweet Misty
I wish your eyes weren't so sad
Sure times got pretty bad
You have to remember you weren't driving the car
I know you still spent a few years behind bars

Oh sweet Misty
I know I wasn't there but I wish you could see your light
It wasn't your decision to make that night
Regardless you paid your debt
And the loss of life isn't something you forget

Oh sweet Misty
You've been doing well
A couple of years since you touched the old needle
But I still have to remember your smile
It's not something I've seen in a while

Oh sweet Misty
Stop beating yourself up
It's a long time since you were drowning in that old loving cup
As much as you want it clocks don't tend to turn back
If I could I'd make it happen and that's a fact

CRAZY EYES

There was a guy
We called him Crazy Eyes
Because
Well
He had crazy eyes
I mean that with affection
They both went in different directions
He also wore women's clothes
Told us we were the only people that know
We weren't
People have eyes
They could see what he was wearing
But I'm trying to paint a picture for you to understand
He was a unique kind of man
I met him in Santa Monica
While some dude was playing the harmonica
He came up to me
Started talking about poetry
I gave him a smoke
And a can of coke
We sat and talked
Then he said we should walk
Went from speaking on Hemingway
To Jack London
Humphrey Bogart
And Faye Dunaway
To taps on all our cell phones

And the streets being full of clones
Said that he's been sent
Sent with a mission to prevent
A clone takeover
I was lost for words
Sounded absurd
But he was wearing women's bell bottoms
A bikini top and an over coat
The promenade was just a place I'd go
But that street was his home
He said some of the wisest words
But he also said some of the dumbest shit I've ever heard
Like once he gave his insight
Into reading Oscar Wilde
He spoke on the imagery
And made his own analogies
He said mankind was like Dorian Gray
Losing itself in its own vanity
That was an example of the wiser words
But it's only fair to illustrate the absurd
One day we were talking on the street
A street patrol was walking the beat
Sees Crazy Eyes' belongings
Said they were in a place they don't belong
Officer told him to move the bag from the street
I thought it was all a bit unnecessary
It was just a bag you know
Where else should it go
He's sleeping out in the cold

But the officer was persistent
Then Crazy Eyes became indignant
Started screaming pretty hard
"FUCK YOU! YOU BLACK BASTARD"
The officer stood in awe
Like he'd never seen insanity before
Crazy Eyes then walked over to me
And I'm still in a little disbelief
He said to me
"Who is more in control?
The one that remains calm
Or the one who screams and bawls?"
I said "the one who remains calm
Is more likely to prevent harm"
He said "exactly
So did you see me
Talking to that fool
And not once did I lose my cool"
I thought to myself
It's not just his eyes that are crazy
But this was a man that believed
I swear
I was going to tell Crazy Eyes
I thought he was wrong
But then I remembered he thought most of us were clones

What the fuck was I supposed to do?

THE BALLAD OF WHISKEY AND WEED

Whiskey thought he had a clear head
But his lip had started to snarl and his temper to flare
He was sensitive to every word that was said
So Whiskey left the bar to get some air
Not knowing who he was going to meet out there
He burst out of the door
Trying his best not to care
But with Whiskey less is less and more is more

Sat in a booth Weed tried to stay awake
Her friends were talking nonsense all night
She didn't know how much more she could take
So she stepped outside in search of a light
That's when she saw Whiskey ready to fight
She was pretty quick to calm him down
Sometimes love happens at first sight
Whiskey watched Weed walk the aisle in her wedding gown

She always remained pretty chilled
Occasionally he was prone to shout
Alone they had different kinds of will
But together they figured it out
But it didn't seem a sustainable route
They began to depend on each other
Then came an emotional drought
Led them to finding other lovers

All good things must come to an end
They both went their separate ways
But they remain good friends
I heard they still see each other most days

LET'S GET STONED

When I was a kid
Teachers said
I wasn't paying attention
They said I always seemed to have something else on my mind
I was always listening
Always watching
And observing
I don't ever think I'm right about anything
It's amazing what can be found
When you just look around
I'm not trying to be profound
I'm just finding a way to say my thoughts out loud
I see today
And see we're totally plagued
Fake news and social med-I-A
I'm running out of words to say
Losing my voice
Screaming over the noise
Hard not to be annoyed
When every topic is a topic to avoid
I see the agendas
And the repeat offenders
My thoughts are in a blender
But the time to fight is the time you're ready to surrender
I'm tired
Of our leaders being liars

So I'm following my heart's desires
I'm going to smoke this bowl until I get higher
And I won't pretend
I won't smoke again
Because once it's smoked
I'll load another one
I've just had enough
So
Let's all get stoned

THE GHOST OF PEG ENTWISTLE

I'm hiking to the Hollywood sign
Sun is shining and I'm feeling fine
I just want to get as close as I can
Touch the sign with my hands
But it has no civilian access
So I'm forced to trespass
Sign used to read Hollywoodland
After a real estate development
The sun was starting to set
And I was starting to forget
I have to walk back
But I've already left the beaten track
Eventually the 'H' I'm able to touch
All of a sudden
I feel a rush
I must start climbing
Keep on climbing
I'm not minding
Just want to keep on climbing
Climb to the top of the 'H'
I'd been wanting to do this for a lot of days
All of a sudden
I see a skeleton face
And I feel an incredible bump
As Peg Entwistle tells me to jump
What else am I supposed to do?
After that shitty movie review

My career too seems surely through
So the ghost of Peg Entwistle takes my hand
And into the night we flew

THE HOLLYWOOD NO SHOES BLUES

I'd been surfing couches
I rode the waves
Like there was no yesterday
But I was finally
Moving into my own place
I'd spent the day
Putting together furniture from I kee A
When I say
Furniture
I mean a bed frame
But my friend came
Helped me put it together
Then to celebrate
I opened a bottle of wine
Poured each other a glass
Told my friend
I didn't want to be an ass
But I wanted to go outside to smoke
He said he'd put his boots on
I said no need
We're just going out front
But he was dressed in all black
Apart from his socks
His socks were white
He said that wasn't right
On went his boots
I went out in my socks

One pink and one blue
Didn't match
And had holes in the soles
But I'd become attached
I also didn't have many others
I didn't care
It wasn't like we were planning to go anywhere
After our smoke
We head back inside
To be reunited with our wine
Finished our glasses
Poured another
It was time for another cigarette
I was allowed to smoke inside
But I didn't want to
Sure
Eventually that's what I'd do
After I lived there a day or two
But I hadn't even slept there a single night
So we stood outside in the moonlight
This particular time
My friend didn't worry about his boots
Didn't want the ordeal of going through
The whole process of tying laces
I didn't blame him
We're both stood on the stoop in our socks
But I forgot
An important part of smoking out front
It is essential for re-admittance

To remember the keys
Because the doors lock automatically
It was too late to call the landlord
I mean
I'd just picked up the keys that day
I thought I could maybe stay
At my friend's place
But he also
Left his keys in my place
We didn't quite know what to do
We had a classic case of
The Hollywood no shoes blues

I had my wallet
And not much else
So we walked
To the local bar
Our friend was working
The regulars were lurking
Said their hellos
Told us their stories
They didn't even realize
We were without shoes
Everyone's caught up in their own news
Trapped believing their own views
I suppose we all have our own kinds of
The Hollywood no shoes blues

Our friend closed the bar
Put us in his car
Like we needed a babysitter
He took us to buy slippers
At a Rite Aid
At 4am
Then we went back with him
To wait until
The landlord would let us in
He laid out sheets on his couch
And brought an air mattress out
Put it on the floor
And poured whiskey for us all
Each in a glass quite tall
We sat on his porch
He went to bed around seven
We finished the bottle around nine
Figured that was a good time
To see if we were able to get back into mine
But we weren't walking in a straight line
As we arrived
We saw the landlord outside
He let us inside
We were once again
Reunited with our glasses of wine
Figured we may as well finish it all
When his friend decided to call
Said he was feeling pretty rough
And was slightly down on his luck

Wondered if we wanted to get lunch
Well
We hadn't eaten
So we figured why not
I went to put on my shoes
When my friend grabbed my shoe
It was at this point he threw
Threw my shoe
Across the room
Picked up my other shoe
Then he threw that too
I was confused
He said he started to like
The Hollywood no shoes blues

Now he was wearing slippers
Instead of his boots
He exclaimed that "SLIPPERS RULE"
So off we went
To buy tuna melts
In our slippers
The friend that picked us up
The one that was feeling rough
And down on his luck
Said he felt better when he saw us
He said "at least I'm doing better than you"
I suppose some people don't quite understand

The just moved into a place walking around Los Angeles in slippers
Hollywood no shoes blues

HEAVY HEARTS & EMPTY GLASSES

I have worries on my mind
Troubles trailing behind
All the sorrow you can find

Heavy hearts and empty glasses
Blood thicker than molasses
Drinking this bar dry you bet your asses

Whiskey till the feeling dissipates
Which is normally when the features start to sway
And nothing appears straight

The ground is cold
I'm holding onto the floor
Like I'm hanging from a trap door

Waiting for the audience to go
But this is no stage show
There's nothing to break my fall

It's okay I understand
There doesn't seem to be a place to land
Just free falling for as long as I can

EVERYTHING IS OKAY

An astounding amount of people read self-help books
An astonishing number of people are completely fucked
But everyone has their secrets of life to sell
They're all over the bookshelves
People buy them and pass them along
Till the next one tells them they're wrong
They told me visualization was the answer
Who the fuck visualized cancer?
I was told to place a cosmic order
But there's still people raping our sons and daughters
They told me God listens whenever I pray
He just answers prayers in his own way
God should work at Starbucks
I went in there today
Ordered an Americano they gave me a latte
I'm just trying to say
Everything is okay
I have it all figured out
This is now
Officially a self-help book
So
If your life kinda sucks
Give me some of your wages
And the answers will be locked in the pages
Prepare yourselves
The secret to life is at hand
And this is all you and I need to understand

I truly believe this is the secret to all of it
We don't know diddly shit
None of us
Especially me
No clue
No idea
I'm just happy to be here

JOSEPH SMITH

The ghost of Joseph Smith appeared to me
He came in a dream
Told me to share what I had seen
Tell the whole world
He was full of shit and he married little girls

THE HOOKER WITH A HEART OF GOLD

As all legends tend to go
The full story may never be known
But as they say
Rosa May
Made her way
From New York City to Colorado
To Virginia City but not before Idaho
Then there was Carson City and Reno
Then she ended up in Bodie
Californ-I-A
According to the legend of Rosa May
They say she never left
Before succumbing to her death
Rosa was a working girl
Making men's toes curl
Moving from brothel to brothel
To the Red-Light District of Bodie
She settled there in 1893
In that old mining town
Which was transformed when they found
Gold in the ground
Made it into a wild west boomtown
Now it's nothing but a ghost town
But they reckon Rosa stuck around
During its decline
Nursing the sick that worked in the mine
During a sickness epidemic

She became a make shift medic
They say the illness killed her
At least that's what I was told
She was around sixty years old
Bodie was windy with a subarctic cold
Some would say God broke his mold
The day
God made
Rosa May
The people say
She was the hooker with a heart of gold

MISSING PEOPLE

Missing people
Missing boys and girls
Unanswered questions
Devastated parents
A fucked up world
Missing men and missing women
Tortured victims
Lost friends and family
Missing people
Murder in the air
Missing persons everywhere
A fucked up world
Stealing people
Stealing lives
Stealing breath
Murder tonight
Final breaths captured in fear
Too many people missing
Too many stories we'll never hear
Stories of the missing people
The ones that disappeared

SADNESS IS MY SHADOW

Sadness is my shadow
Everywhere I go
Has been since I was just a couple of years old
Every word I've spoken
Every joke I've told
Sadness has been my shadow
I was just a child
Trying to make people smile
I'm still trying to enjoy this ride
But I still have sadness by my side
Even when I first fell in love
It still didn't feel enough
I was waiting to lose any trust
Waiting for the passion to rust
Eventually we all go bust
Sand under my feet today
Swimming in the ocean waves
But my shadow stays
The sun may shine
But she's there all the time
I'm learning not to mind
And I occasionally find shade sometimes
But like lifelines
Forgotten rhymes
And reckless tides
Sadness stays by my side
At the christening

Everyone was listening
Water on the head glistening
Sadness is my shadow
When the phone rings
When the singer sings
I feel the joy it brings
But I also feel other things
I feel a heart break
I feel faith shake
I see hate for the sake
And a waterless lake
A world that takes
The tape's going on
And a television program
Can only last so long
Before the audience has gone
What's wrong?
Turn off the TV show
We've all seen the episode
And the plot I know
I'm out here
Trying to put ducks in a row
But it's hard to tell the best place for each one to go
When sadness is still my shadow

CALIFORNIA

California
The Golden State
Been north to Klamath
And south to Chula Vista
Mount Whitney
Sierra Nevada
Sequoia National Forest
Redwood trees
Mariposa County
Yosemite
Big Bear Lake
San Jose
Not to mention Monteray
And Grizzly Bay
Oh Californ-I-A
A boy was born in Fresno
Off to university he would go
He moved down south to San Diego
Get his parents off his back
He never particularly liked math
But it was a test he passed
He got a job
At a retail store
Selling clothes
Soon enough
He didn't want to go to university anymore
But twenty-two years before

A girl was born
Up north in Sacramento
After her parents divorced
She moved with her mom
From the north
To be near family in City Heights
She got a job at a retail store
Selling clothes
That's how they met
She was desperate for more
He was happy to get along
She had a particular passion
She'd always been fascinated by fashion
Nobody knows
Why he wanted to sell clothes
Just needed a job I suppose
She applied to fashion schools
She decided it was something she had to do
Time passed as she waited to hear
They had fallen in love
The way only a young couple could
Then in the mail a letter came
Reading her name
She opened it up
She was moving to LA
Otis College of Art and Design
They transferred their jobs
To a store in Santa Monica
Rented a small apartment

Where they both would live
But city living is expensive
She worked and studied a lot
He got a second job
She was top of her class
He was watching the time pass
But they were determined to make their love last
He started to come home late
She started spending more time with her classmates
He eventually got a job at the bar he'd been drinking in
And she was thinking about leaving him
But for a little while they started to breathe again
When they decided to spend
The entire weekend
At a cottage in Crystal Cove
Off they drove
They were swimming
Walking
Hiking
Shared a few cocktails
Taking in
The Californian
Beaches
And all of their features
The ocean spraying
Children playing
She was set to graduate
Got offered a job up in San Francisco
He asked when they had to go

So he would know
How long it would take
Before they were to relocate
To San Francisco Bay
She told him to stay
Then came
The time for them to separate
Off she flew
To pastures new
Before he could think what to do
He started to drink a lot
Working and paying rent he forgot
Eventually the landlord took back the lot
He was forced to go
Tail between his legs
Back to Fresno
Old friends
His parent's basement
Got a job at a dive bar
But he put his paycheck back into the place
He was wearing the years on his face
She was following her dreams
Job paying her a lot of money
Working for some fancy fashion company
Where money and success goes
Excess often seems to follow
She was a leading lady in this show
But the money started making its way up her nose
Every weekend

And before too long
Weekends turned to weeknights
And the weekdays she had to pretend
Everything was going alright
Her habit increasing
She got in her car
After too many drinks at the bar
The cops pulled her over
Somewhere near Fisherman's Wharf
Work didn't fire her but gave her time off
So she could get clean
Traded jail for a rehab facility
Northeast in Napa Valley
On her third day
She saw a man shaking away
She remembered him
From San Diego to LA
Remembered telling him to stay
It had been a few years
They were both looking a little worse for wear
He couldn't believe it when he saw her
They embraced
When they came face to face
In that clinical place
In ol' Californ-I-A
Coastal roads
The Mammoth snow
Beauty seems to be everywhere you go
He briefly stopped back in Fresno

Before getting himself to his feet
Went back to finish his degree
Till he was wearing a suit working in Silicon Valley
She went back to the fashion industry
Even though she continued to stay clean
She couldn't seem to flee her misery
She wasn't sure what her life would mean
Or even if it was going to mean anything
As the years rolled on
He married a woman
Had two kids
He spent most of his days in the office
Thinking it wasn't the life he was promised
The divorce wasn't final
But the papers were signed
His wife moved the kids
To live near her family
Close to Santa Barbara
He opened the bottle
And didn't stop
Till he was standing atop
Of the Golden Gate Bridge
Some way to go
Doctors had already said
He only had a few months to go
At the young age of fifty-four
Meanwhile she continued to grow old
Left fashion behind
In order to find

A quieter time
She moved to Carmel by the Sea
Spent the rest of her days working in a small art gallery
Lived through her eighties
Never got married
But most that met her said she was happy
I suppose it's hard to say
Californ-I-A
Grains of sand
On the golden land
Sink or swim
She has everything
Every story has a beginning and an end
In 1987 the California Condor
Was in the wild no more
Like the Condor
On we must go
Some love stories have a beginning
A middle
And an end
But I can't pretend
To know anything about love
I haven't seen it as much
So when it comes to love's curious case
I'll be listening to the stories whispered in the winds
Of good ol' Californ-I-A

NOT NOW

Not now
Not anytime
Not yesterday
Not today
Or tomorrow
I said
Not now
Not ever
Not whenever
Not together
Not now
Not ever

THE COFFEE IN MY CUP IS COLD

The coffee in my cup is cold
It might be a few hours old
My cigarette is barely lit
I've hardly been smoking it
The newspaper is open on page one
And I can no longer read on
My eggs are untouched
I knew I couldn't eat much
The gas in my car is lower than low
Battery's dead and I don't know whether
She should be scrapped or towed
It's raining beyond these walls
And the soles of my shoes are covered in holes
My head can't think
My pen's out of ink
I'm writing a song to sing
On a guitar with broken strings
Feels like I'm waiting for water to turn into steam
Only to try to make steam turn back to water and then to make it freeze
I can navigate the maze
But I get lost when the roads are straight
I don't know whether to hang up or hold
But the coffee in my cup is cold

YOU DON'T KNOW ME AT ALL

You think you know me
When you don't know shit at all
I'm always swinging
When my back's against the wall
You think I'm sat alone
Waiting on you to call
Tomorrow I'm waking in someone else's bed
You don't need to break my fall
Let him kiss you goodnight
I'll have a Jack & Coke make it a highball
Actually make it a Jack & ginger
You don't know me at all

IT'S BEEN A WHILE SINCE I'VE BEEN TO ANY KIND OF CHURCH

It's been a while since I've been to any kind of church
Standing inside those buildings only seems to hurt
I've fallen asleep in services all over the world
There's been many a choir I have heard
I pretended to listen to all of the priest's words
But I always found most of those words to be absurd
I found a lot of the people to be disturbed
Not everyone but enough to be perturbed
It's been a while since I've been in any kind of church

There was a Korean church next to my place
Over on Edgemont East Hollywood way
We'd go over there with a basketball to play
Outside they had some hoops that stayed
Sometimes we'd have to wait all day
Until most the parked cars went away
It was used as a parking lot during the day
And I'll be the first to say
Don't blame me if your car is hit with a basketball if you
parked that car under a basketball hoop
What the fuck else was I going to do?
But apart from that we never used the church

Me and a friend of mine
Had been drinking a little wine
We were both feeling pretty fine
If you have an hour or two

I'd like to share a story with you
I was crashing with this girl I knew
The other side of the 101
My friend was told by his girlfriend
Not to get too drunk
Because in the morning
We were all going to drive to Mount Wilson
No reason
Just for fun
But it's something
We'd all frequently done
My friend's girlfriend was having dinner with the girl I was staying with
While me and her boyfriend watched the basketball
Playoffs
Having a glass of wine
A very sophisticated time
The game was over
So was the wine
All four bottles
But it was okay
There was a bar down the street
We stayed until close
Found a liquor store
And split a fifth
My phone was on silent
His phone had died
Turned out his girlfriend started to worry if we were alive
She called up the girl I was staying with

To see if we were there
We weren't
So she came to find us
And let's just say
It wasn't our proudest day
And she didn't have the nicest things to say
When she eventually found us
Sitting in the doorstep of a church
Sharing a joint
Splitting the whiskey
Listening to the Stones
Sympathy for the Devil
We were fucked
Mount Wilson sucked
But it's been a while since I've been to any kind of church

Although there was this one time
I attended the church of John Prine
Every song ageing like a fine wine
And the new ones were ahead of their time
I can only hope they'll forever survive
If you ever want to feel alive
Let the preacher preach on his signs
While you go out and ease your mind
Because happiness is hard to find
But I found happiness in the church of John Prine

CHRISTOPHER DENNIS

Kirk Alyn played Superman
In 1948 and in 1950
He was a dancer
That leapt gracefully off his feet
George Reeves
Played Superman on TV
During most of the fifties
In the seventies
They made *Superman: The Movie*
With a man named
Christopher Reeve
Most say he's the best Superman there's ever been
But he wasn't quite the best for me
Sure he was great and he played the part
To pick the person that is Superman for me
I'd have to answer honestly
And the decision isn't too hard
There was a guy called Christopher Dennis
He used to walk on Hollywood Boulevard
Posing and taking photos for tips
Making the days of many tourists
He was in a movie called *Confessions of a Superhero*
Even appeared on *Kimmel* before
Dennis once uttered the truest words spoken
When he said
"Hollywood is a place where dreams are made and dreams are broken"

He flew higher and higher
But unlike the Man of Steel's flight
Some highs are just the other end of a light
Even Superman has his kryptonite
He lost his home
His costume was stolen
Pan handling
Life gambling
Bottom of the barreling
Eventually
He raised some money
Bought a new suit
Life was back on track
But it's easy to fall back
Before too long he seemed to crack
But when he put on that suit
He brought smiles to faces
His picture has been shown in many places
Every time he seemed to fall
Have his back up against the wall
He grabbed onto his laces
Pulled himself up
But Christopher Dennis had run out of luck
He was laid to rest
Buried in his Superman vest
I don't know if all the stories are true
But Hollywood was certainly a part of you
Superman was maybe the rest of you
You became him

Wearing the red
Yellow
And blue
Hollywood doesn't quite know what to do
I mean you were a part of her too
Found in the valley at the age of 52
When people say Superman's name
They may be talking about Tim Daly or Dean Cain
Bud Collyer
Henry Cavill
Or Tyler Hoechlin
Brandon Routh
Mark Harmon
Or Tom Welling
There's too many names to list
So many *Supermans* there's one I'm sure to miss
But when I think about Superman
I think about Christopher Dennis

WHO AM I TALKING TO?

Who am I talking to?
I know it's you
But which one of your faces am I talking to?
The one saying I love you
Or the one saying fuck you?

You're talking to me
The girl of your dreams
The girl that is everything she's trying to be
The one saying you love me
And I love you too
You see?

I see and I've been meaning to talk to you
It didn't quite seem we were through
And there's a lot that I've been trying to do
I guess I'm saying I love you
Maybe I always loved you

That's so sweet
But you couldn't possibly believe
When I said I was the girl of your dreams
I was trying to deceive
Thought it would be pretty funny
It might be true that you love me
But I was always the girl saying fuck you
You see?

HEAVEN'S GATE

Phenobarbital and apple sauce
Washed down with vodka of course
Plastic bags over their heads
Believing only the body would be dead
That a UFO
Was going to take their souls
Through the gates of Heaven
All dressed in uniform
All to die before too long
Marshall Applewhite
Believed when Bonnie Nettles died
She was taken inside
A spacecraft
Comet Hale-Bopp was set to arrive
Prompting Marshall to lead the mass suicide

ANOTHER WEDDING DAY

The morning was bright
As I sat with my coffee
Watching the dawn provide the first light
But for some reason
Unknown to me
I felt like I was waking in a dream

The rain started to fall
It began to pour
Not just a little
It was set for the long haul
That's when I found out the news
I was a little amused
To hear you said your "I do's" too

You see I wrote a poem
Called it *Wedding Day*
Without even knowing
In fact I had another girl in mind
I always knew old lovers would find new ones
Guess this is the year for getting those contracts signed

It's raining today
I'm going for a walk
Sure it'll go away but I want the rain to stay
It just seems to make sense
Not because I'm melancholy
I'm well aware me and you or you and I
We don't exist together in the present tense

Maybe I was a fool for hoping
That you'd always be a part of my life in some way
I suppose I'll leave the door open
I wasn't expecting an invite
But I was hoping to hear it from you
And not from a drunk in a bar one night

I'm wet inside and out
But my cigarette manages to light
As smoke circulates my doubts
My feet are soaked
And I've been going back and forth
Fighting with my back against the ropes

You don't owe me anything
I mean that sincerely
So if I call
Let it ring
But I want you to know
I do intend
To live up to the promise
That you can always call me your friend

I don't mean we go for coffee dates
Or hang out at bars till late
Just occasional updates
Let each other know we're doing okay
I suppose I'm trying to say
Although it's raining here today
The sun is shining your way
And as long as that stays the case
I'll happily walk in the rain the rest of my days

REDLINE PART 2

I was on the redline
Somewhere near Pershing Square
I was headed north of there
When this guy sat down near me
Put his hands in his underwear
And all of a sudden
His dick was out
There wasn't too many people about
Thank God
I didn't know what to do
I moved seats
You meet all kinds of people on the redline

JUNKIES

Empty the bank account
Put it in my arm
It's the only thing keeping me calm
I'm just a junkie
Fucking scum of the earth
What's my life worth?

Empty the bank account
Put it on a horse
I've had a tip and it's my lucky racecourse
I'm just a junkie
With this gambling curse
What's my life worth?

Empty the bank account
And fill me with liquor
I couldn't possibly be any sicker
I'm just a junkie
Let's toast my journey to the hearse
What's my life worth?

Empty the bank account
We'll have another child
Maybe that will keep us together for a while
I'm just a junkie
Hoping love's real and it works
What's my life worth?

Empty the bank account
I want it all to myself
All of my incredible wealth
I'm just a junkie
Tax free of course
What's my life worth?

Empty the bank account
Give it all away
I'm tired of money ruling everything today
We're all junkies
In our own ways
Fixin' on making mistakes
We want to feel love
We try to feel hate
What the fuck is this life worth?

ONE OF THOSE DAYS

It had been a long day
Needless to say
I was not in the mood
To deal with this dude
He was holding a bat
With nails attached
Shouting at this guy
Waving his stick in the sky
I'll start from the top
I was woken that day by a knock
At about seven o'clock
It was just old Charlie
Back in the day he used to ride a Harley
Now he spends most of his time in bed
Except when he forgets to take his meds
Then he walks the halls more
And tends to knock on my door
Made him a cup of tea
Made myself a black coffee
Didn't let him in the first time we met
But now he just stays for a few cigarettes
It was Sunday morning
I wasn't expecting to see the day dawning
But there I was
I didn't mind because
My lady was planning to stop by
Just to say 'hi'

Before I had to go to work in the night
Serving people till they blurred their sight
At this old rundown bar
Before I move the story on that far
My girlfriend arrived
Like a vision for my sore eyes
Things were looking up
She was so beautiful
I couldn't believe my luck
I said to her "Darling
I love you much"
She said "that's sweet
We need to break up"
Told you guys my day sucked
Off to work I went
I didn't need an argument
The punters had been emptying their cups
They were already drunk when I showed up
They'd been watching football
It did kick off at 10am after all
A fight broke out in the parking lot
We let it go till it stopped
My pay was supposed to be in the safe
My boss tells me I'll have to wait a few more days
We closed at two and I left at three
Went to this place for a bite to eat
I wanted to be left alone
So I ordered my food to take home
Heard this lady crying to a waitress

Who said she'd call the police
Quite clearly
I'd walked into a situation
As the police were supposedly leaving the station
Heard her say her husband was still outside
Looking after their belongings while a guy was threatening his life
Man
Life's tough living on the streets
I recognized them from the bus stop where they usually sleep
I saw a guy holding a bat
With nails attached
Shouting at this guy
Waving his weapon into the sky
Everyone was staring
Staring doesn't help so I stepped outside
Told the guy I just wanted to say
The police were on their way
So maybe he should go
But no
He didn't seem to mind
So I decided to try and kill some time
It seemed more like meth than coke
I offered him a smoke
He took it and lit her up
That's when I saw a police car stop
They were across the street
I expected them to head over

But they stayed in their seats
LAPD
No implication intended
But it's a force that could be mended
They get out and walk in the 7/11
Meanwhile this guy's still waving around his goddamn weapon
The waitress got the police's attention
So they put the big gulps in the squad car
Don't want to spill their soda
On the front seat I saw them put
A bag of what could only be a sugary treat
Next thing I know
All three of us are laid on the floor
Police had their guns drawn
The day was already too many hours old
And my tuna melt was sure to be fucking cold
But that night I went back to my place to dwell
The homeless couple slept wherever their heads fell
And the guy with the bat spent the night in the cell
I suppose someone is always having a worse day than you

JUMBO'S CLOWN ROOM

There's pictures of clowns covering the walls
One stage and a solitary pole
A bar and that's all it's quite small
And the ceiling is pretty damn low
Over at Jumbo's

The girls are sweet
But if you're mean
It won't keep them keen
Might even leave you bleeding at the spleen
Down at old Jumbo's

They dance to thrill
So bring all your bills
And they'll dance until
Your wallets need to be refilled
Come on down to Jumbo's

There's a line out front
But I was told she'd let me in whenever I want
She danced till one
Then we went back out front and shared a blunt
That particular night at Jumbo's

You don't have to wait till dark
They have girls all day that can break your heart
While you let reality depart
This isn't the place to bite or bark
This is Jumbo's

Whether you are a soon to be groom
Or your love life seems totally doomed
For whatever reason I can presume to assume
They have a girl waiting to dance for you
Just get your ass down to Jumbo's Clown Room

STREET CORNER

I'm standing on this street corner
Been here since the morning
I got a job working for the press
Said they'd give me a test
Said I must pass
These jobs are competitive
Told me if I failed they'd give me hell
They gave me a bunch of fear to sell
One of the guys
Wearing a shirt and a tie
Handed me an entire bundle of fear
Told me to get rid of this on this street corner here
I was told I must sell each piece
For five dollars each
I made my way to this here corner at 10am
I've been standing here since then
Needless to say
I didn't start today
With much hope at all
Who wants to pay for fear after all
I couldn't believe my eyes
I was totally surprised
Fear was flying off the shelf
Man
It was selling itself
Like you wouldn't believe
I was on my tenth bundle by three

They thought I'd only need one
Boy they were wrong
They we're hoping I'd get demoted
But the boss asks me if I want to be promoted
Offers me a deal
Over some swanky meal
Asks me
If I'd like to be on TV
Said someone like me they could really use
To sell some fear on this thing called the news
I said I never really came here
To sell any kind of fear
But he supposes that's where the money is
And that's just basic business
I never was too good with business
I quit
Now I'm sitting on that street corner

MOTHERFUCKER

The word motherfucker can be used in many ways
I'd like to demonstrate
It can be used to compliment
It can be used to intimidate
Shit
People use the word to masturbate
There's a lot of weird shit on the internet
I digress
So let me address
The word motherfucker
If I refer to someone as "my motherfucker"
I'm talking about a friend
If I say to someone "you motherfucker"
I could be saying it about a friend
Maybe he did something dumb
And that's my way of saying don't do it again
But you really need to read the intent
And be sure to put the phrase in context
Because if we've just met
And I'm shouting "you motherfucker"
We might not be friends
So I suppose it all depends
On many things
You have to use your judgment
If I'm heard saying "this motherfucker"
I could once again
Be referring to a dumbass friend

Or it could be uttered through gritted teeth
About some guy I don't want to see
And never wanted to meet
Motherfucker is a word of rich complexity
It can even be spelt differently
Sure motherfucker is normal
But it seems crude and offensively formal
Muthafukah
Muthafucker
Muthafuckah
Whatever spelling you wish to see
They may not be in the dictionary
And the spelling may be make-believe
But we'll know what you mean
Besides if you want to be a bad motherfucker
Bad Motherfuckers only do as they please

COFFIN or THE LIVING DEAD or WE ALL DIE, SO LET'S NOT KILL OURSELVES WHILE WE'RE STILL LIVING or LEAVING FLOWERS AT MY GRAVE or RYAN REYNOLDS IN THAT ONE MOVIE, THE ONE, WHERE HE WAS BURIED FOR THE ENTIRE MOVIE, I MEAN, I RESPECT THE COMMITMENT, LIKE WHEN CHRISTIAN BALE LOST WEIGHT FOR THE MACHINIST, BY ONLY DRINKING WATER, EATING ONE APPLE, DRINKING COFFEE WITH THE ODD WHISKEY IN ORDER TO LOSE WEIGHT FOR THE ROLE. MEANWHILE, ADAM SANDLER IS SHOOTING A FILM IN HAWAII AND I DON'T KNOW WHICH I ADMIRE MORE, THIS NO LONGER HAS ANYTHING TO DO WITH WHAT IS WRITTEN NEXT.

I'm laid in a coffin
My eyes are sewn shut
My body is rotting
From my head to my foot
But if I won't wake up
How can I expect anyone to give a fuck?

It's dark in this casket
But my mind is at ease
I was too young to be past it
I'm finally at peace
I was also tired of trying to deceive
Only ever wanted to believe

I hear people leaving flowers at my grave
But I seem to have no more words left to say
No energy to wave

So here I lay
Laying here today
As I did yesterday
Maybe eventually everything will be okay
Perhaps it is already
But from down here
It seems pretty heavy

I FELL IN LOVE IN THE MUSÉE D'ORSAY

I fell in love in the Musée d'Orsay
They had so much art on display
Through every room
I began to make my way
I'd run out of words to say
When I came across Claude Monet
Train dans la Champagne
It seemed like it was painted for me
Like the *Champ de coquelicots*
Environs de Giverney
I was on some kind of journey
Experiencing
The *Bras se Seine près de Giverney*
But little did I know
I was about to be taken away by Van Gogh
La nuit étoilée
I fell in love in the Musée d'Orsay
I was waiting
The time had come to leave
But my eyes truly didn't deceive
Because that's the moment I first saw true beauty
She was staring right back at me
My jaw fell on down to my feet
After all the beauty I'd seen
Standing in front of me was an artist's dream
I had to leave
She had to leave

But all was okay
I'd never seen true beauty until that day
When I fell in love with the girl standing across from me in the Musée d'Orsay

I was at the Guggenheim tonight
The gallery was designed by Frank Lloyd Wright
I wanted to see some work by Jackson Pollock
They were displaying *The Moon Woman* and *Eyes in the Heat*
Enchanted Forest and *Alchemy*
They also had *Ocean Greyness* and *Circumcision*
So I made the decision
To make my way
Up the winding stairway
Stopping by John Chamberlain
And a new exhibition
Also stopped by Solomon's Founding Collection
So much beauty for selection
They asked me as I was leaving
If I could fill out a survey about my experience
I said the selection was great
And I'd had a very special day
I was honest
And it was hard to say
Because they were holding some of my favorite strokes of paint
But none of them contained your face
So I could only say I liked it

And I hope that's okay
The Guggenheim does remain
A special place to me
To this very day
But l liked it
Is all I can say
Because I fell in love with you in the Musée d'Orsay

OVERWORKED & UNDERPAID

I've been working all day
Trying to get paid
4am I would awake
Took the bus out to the Promenade
6am I was ready to start
Not saying the work is hard
Unpacking boxes folding clothes by day
By night I'm tending bar
Then I'd start again
Six or seven days a week
But it ain't the blast furnace like my great granddaddy
I'm not trying to complain
All I'm trying to say
Is that eighty plus hours should be able to pay
My rent today
But like last month it's going to be late
I suppose that's the price you pay
Living in the city
But I'm not exaggerating when I tell you my place is shitty
Ground floor
The roaches don't use the door
Most nights police are called
Domestic disturbance and the occasional raid
I'm not trying to be a millionaire
I mean I don't really care
Fancy clothes tend to fade
Watches tend to break

Fine food eventually turns to waste
I'm tired of wasting my days
Being overworked and underpaid

DOWN AT THE POOL HALL

Today is a good day
I'm going down to the pool hall to play
I'm meeting my friend there
It's been a while since she and I played
I think the last time we played
I was *in between places*
And it was a friend of mine's birthday
I've played a lot of pool over the years
Started playing a lot
When I sobered up
There was a pool table in a coffee shop
So me and a couple of friends
Would drink coffee
Smoke cigarettes
And play pool till the days end
I met a guy
Swear to God
He was good
He was able to pot any ball he wanted
Showed me how to pot the black on the break
He could make the cue ball
Hang in the air before it would fall
And land on the eight
Slicing the top of it
Sending her
To whichever pocket
He wanted

Automatic win
We'd play again
I wasn't much for beating him
If you missed a shot
He was sure to win
He taught me a thing or two about hustling
He didn't recommend it
But we all get desperate
I'm going to the pool hall today
One time
I was shooting pool with my friend
I called him Big Ben
Because he was small
And always late
Sometimes nicknames mean the opposite
This old timer
Put down a quarter
Wanted to play winner
Which between me and Benny
Well
I don't mean to brag
But the winner between me and Benny
Was usually me
This was
No different
So I racked up the balls
I broke them up
Potted a couple
Till I rode my luck

And the ball span too much
The old timer stepped up
Arthritis
He had it bad
I could see it in his hands
He wasn't able to steady the cue
Because his left arm
He couldn't use
So he rested the cue against the table
To try and keep the movement stable
Well he was certainly able
Because in the next seven shots
He sank the lot
Then made the eight
Corner pocket
On his final shot
Taught me a lot
I played him a few times since
I still can't win
Today should be a good day
I'm going down to the pool hall to play
I was in a bar up in Harlem
Played against a guy named Champ
I was holding my own
Because I'd gotten pretty good y'know
He didn't have a clear shot
But he spun the ball
In a way I've never seen before
After he won

No one
Had money on the table
So I asked
If he had the time
And didn't mind
Could he show me how he won
When he spun
The ball so fine
Shit
He taught me a bunch of cool tricks
And I eventually beat him in a game
But I'll always respect his name
We never played for money
Nor did me and LT
When LT played
The balls went wherever he wanted them to be
No one fucked with LT
I always remember him telling me
One particular day he was playing badly
Still beating me
But told me
He did just see
A young woman
Leap to her death
From the top of his Projects
The Bronx
New York City
I'm talking 11212 and not the 10463
Brownsville

Not the house of the Kennedy's
Anyway
Me and LT
Were shooting some pool
He taught me
How to make life easy
By leaving the cue ball wherever I needed it to be
Same bar
There was a guy called Johnny
He once threw the cue ball directly at me
Threw it
First time I beat him
Sure
We were friends
And he hugged me
When I found the cue ball again
Today's working out
My old friend's about
She's got the day off
It's been a while for sure
Since we were at that old pool hall
I was in Midtown Manhattan
Found a pool table
In this fancy ass hotel
I was just having a game with a buddy
Taking a second away from our company
This stranger all of a sudden wanted to play me for money
I said no
He said we'd only play for twenty

I said twenty is more than plenty
I didn't care to gamble
I'd had as much hustling as I could handle
Black eyes
Slashed tires
And broken noses
But he kept trying his luck
So I left that night with over a hundred bucks
He tried to threaten me
I didn't give a fuck
I'm no upper Westside schmuck
I'm off to play pool today
Have a few beers and feel okay
I was back in LA
Drunk off my face
Just having a laugh with some friends
Playing doubles
Drinking doubles
Shit
We were
Seeing doubles
When a couple guys wanted to ruffle
A few feathers
Try and cause trouble
Said we weren't very good
I mean
I could barely stand up
But I called his bluff
Told him to step up

One on one
I win
They go away
He wins
I let them stay
Said he could break
That was the last shot he'd take
I cleared the rest of the balls away
And I wouldn't see him again
Ordered a double
Went back to playing doubles
Seeing doubles
Today's pretty cool
'Cos I've always been a fool
For shooting some pool
Solids or stripes
It won't matter tonight
We'll play them all
Down at the pool hall

HORIYOSHI III

I always wanted
A Horiyoshi tattoo
A man by the name
Yoshihito Nakano
Carries on the tradition

DANCING WITH DEATH

I was scared of death
But I became her friend
She danced with me
And I flirted with her
Eventually
We'll be
Together
Forever
Death and I
Death and me
Together for eternity
I've always hated uncertainty
And she certainly
Is the only certainty
I mean
I don't think she's ever been late
Don't think she's ever missed a date
Sometimes I call for her
But she's not there
I'm told she certainly
Knows what's best for me
And eventually
She'll put on her dress for me
And I'll cease to breathe
And we'll dance in my memories

I'M JUST FIGURING THIS SHIT OUT MAN

I'm pissed off
This shit has to stop
I've gone off the deep end
Because I don't want to pretend
That we're not all completely fucked
I may sound like a pessimist
And a pessimist I don't mean to be
But I'm sick to death of this reality
Sick of fake precedents
Being vomited out by posturing presidents
Respected gangsters
And frat house pranksters
I'm tired of keeping quiet
Leaders talking shit and we're all expected to buy it
Empty promises followed by downright lies
And why?
How long until
Those pockets are filled
We're fucking sleepwalking
Because of dumb shit
Like the reality TV
That has us talking
Like what the hell did that whore
Do on the latest episode of *Jersey Shore*
I'm sick of it all
I'm sorry
Don't mean to cause offense

I'll take a written deep breath
I always thought the greatest gift
Was to share happiness
And well I'd be hard pressed
To share more happiness
In this cold dark world
Than a working girl
I never mean to be rude
Nor do I intend to have a bad attitude
But I think it's time to rebel
No violent shit
Don't want to be locked in a cell
What if we all quit our jobs
Every single person
Quits
On the same day
Everyone in the entire world
Just quit
Sure
It would be fun
Although nothing would get done
I mean
Nothing
Anywhere
It would be chaos
Bad idea
But I'm just figuring this shit out man

THE BASTARDS KILLED EMMETT TILL

It was only 1955
The young boy was walking around alive
Visiting family
Deep in Mississippi
Fourteen years old
Nobody really knows
What happened in that store
But it's happened before
They decided which story was right
Based on the storyteller being white
Whether there was a photo
A whistle
Or any words at all
They went to Mose Wright's house to call
They were sure to kill anyone in their way
When they pulled the young boy from Mr Wright's house that day
His body was found in a state that would make the strongest quiver
As they fished young Emmett out of the Tallahatchie River
Beaten
Naked
Unrecognizable
A teenager
Still a boy
Did it make you feel big?
To kill

Young Emmett Till
But surprise
Surprise
The all-white jury
Believed the lies
Well maybe they didn't believe
Maybe even worse
They agreed
It doesn't matter really
They still let the bastards walk
It's hard to seriously talk
Without a sense of irony
About this being the land of the free
You don't have to go too far
To look back
At getting a free pass to murder the blacks
I mean in 1955
Emmett Till died
In 2011 Trayvon Martin was alive
How many people need to die?
1891 they lynched Joe Coe
Then in 1944
Willie James Howard
Gave a white woman a Christmas card
He was fifteen
Forced to jump to his death in the Suwanee
What about in 1906
In Reeves County
Texas

Slab Pitts
Was dragged to death
Then hung
Because he lived with a white woman
1918
Georgia
The lynching of Mary Turner
And her unborn child
She was brave enough to speak out
On the unjust lynchings going about
Upside down
She hung from a tree
Covered in gasoline
They shot her from front to back
But not before
Ripping her child from her stomach
Using a knife
To cut out the child
Before stomping on it
With their white smiles
Now are you telling me
This is a land that sounds free?
It may have been a few years ago
Since the laws of Jim Crow
But there's still blood on the hands
Of the people
Governing these stolen lands
Moving forward seems to be a mystery
But we have to acknowledge the history

Emmett Till
Should never have been killed
But to those that did the killing
The horror sometimes makes people willing
To realize some ideas are insane
Some ideas are deranged
But it takes bravery
To fight for change
Things may have changed today
But they're far from okay
We're nowhere near any destination
But we are on our way
Maybe it's enough to say
I hope
Emmett Till didn't die in vain that day

THE CODEINE BLUES

I'm sick and I'm weak
Stomach's turned outside in
Can't seem to sleep
Tired of suffering

My body is heavy
My mind's in the clouds
Hands far from steady
Standing alone in the middle of a crowd

There's smoke around my head
Ashtray is overflowing
Feet feel like lead
Last time I saw her she was glowing

My bar tab is paid
I've been drinking to the news
That I've caught a case
Of *the codeine blues*

I DON'T WANT TO FALL IN LOVE

I don't want to fall in love
I did it once and that was enough
They say loving is supposed to be tough
But they didn't say it was going to be that rough
Wrapped my heart in handcuffs
I called her bluff
She swallowed the key
Said it wouldn't make its way back to me

I don't want to fall in love
We started as friends
Besides back then she had a boyfriend
Everything that starts must end
As much as I'd love to pretend
My badly broken heart was ready to mend
I just don't believe it to be
It's shattered into pieces scattered at my feet

I don't want to fall in love
Love is sure to bring along pain
And I'm content not feeling it again
I've always preferred heavy clouds to pouring rain
If happiness is the price you pay
I'll do without it for the rest of my days
They say my heart can be fixed for a fee
I say what if I don't want it to be?
Because you see
I don't want to fall in love

4AM CONVERSATIONS

Some conversations
Can only take place at 4am
Can't be repeated again
Let the words remain between friends
Life doesn't break but it bends
Life doesn't have to take but it always ends
My voice was slurred
But I meant every word
It may have seemed absurd
Or the sweetest thing she'd ever heard
But we'd been talking about loss
Speaking on love's steep cost
The mist had turned to frost
Under the moon we were lost
On the porch drinking wine
Sharing our time
Doing the occasional line
And smoking a bowl to feel fine
We were certainly feeling all right
Sometimes darkness reveals the greatest light
Occasionally I'm just short on sight
Her bark certainly wasn't scarier than her bite
But we talked about how we'd grown too old to fight
On that cold New York City night
We talked about how I missed him too
She was twenty-two when she said her I do's
My good friend wasn't great at seeing things through

But she changed him through and through
And sure we'd argue
But I was still the best man
And sure she wasn't my biggest fan
It's no mistake
That I can
Be quite difficult to understand
But because of his demands
Me and her always said we'd do the best we can
And we learned to get along
And now and then we'd even sing the same song
Everyday on his birthday
Me and her
Meet in some sort of way
Reminisce on the old days
Stay up real late
And speak the words that are too hard to say
She didn't really know where to go
You're not supposed to be a widow
At the tender age of twenty-four
The credits ran on his final show
We remembered when she picked me and him up from the police station
Taken in for public intoxication
I see why I was a source of frustration
I was reckless and he gave into temptation
We spoke about her vexation
I remember telling her
They were only allegations

There wouldn't have been any aggravation
Or any sort of altercation
Was it not for the police's botheration
An emotional excavation
No substance in moderation
Just another *4am Conversation*

PACINO & DE NIRO

Did you see *Serpico* with Al Pacino?
Or Robert De Niro in *Casino*?

What about
Taxi Driver "You talkin' to me"
I mean seriously
It's a movie you have to see
Like *Goodfellas*
Deer Hunter
And *The King of Comedy*
A Bronx Tale
Mary Shelley's Frankenstein
Wag the Dog
Jackie Brown
And *Mean Streets*

What about
Scarface when he said "Say hello to my little friend"
That will remain cinema till time ends
True actors make you believe there's no pretend
Like *Carlito's Way*
Donnie Brasco
And *Scent of a Woman*
Dog Day Afternoon
And Justice For All
Cruising
And Scarecrow

The Godfather parts one
Two
And three

In *The Godfather* part two De Niro
played a young Vito Corleone
But Pacino and De Niro didn't share a scene
A scene we'd have to wait until 1995 to see
When Vincent Hanna offered to buy Neil McCauley
A cup of coffee
A movie called *Heat*
Al Pacino and Robert De Niro
Val Kilmer
Jon Voight
And Tom Sizemore
I could list them all
Ashley Judd
And a young Natalie Portman
Dennis Haysbert
William Fichtner
Hank Azaria
And Danny fucking Trejo
So many more to go
Just watch the movie man
Directed by Michael Mann
Put the DVD in and away you go
Watch yourself some Al Pacino
Watch yourself some Robert De Niro
A couple of acting heroes

Filling more seats than the San Siro
Take your seat
Turn off the reality show
Start watching *Heat*
The regrets will be zero
Getting lost in the works of Pacino & De Niro

GUNS COCAINE WHISKEY & WEED

We'd been drinking at Good Times
Beers
Cocktails
Tequila and limes
Six of us headed to an apartment
Over on Beachwood
It belonged to a friend of ours
Thought about a cab to a place open after hours
But then our sixth friend came through the door
Holding a bag of cocaine he found on the barroom floor
Asked if we were ready to have some fun
That's when my friend whose apartment it was pulled out his gun
Don't worry it was in a box
And the box was locked
Well it was locked when he put it on the table
Then he unlocked it
Emptied the chamber
Gun was disabled
Meanwhile my other friend was justifying
Snorting the cocaine he was ready for trying
He said "it's safe
I know all the guys selling out of that place"
He sniffed till his memories were erased
Another friend was fast asleep
Didn't need to count any sheep
My other friend wasn't interested in the gun

Nor was she interested in the Columbian fun
She'd opened up the whiskey
And was grinding her weed
So just to make sure you're keeping track of things
There is my friend to whom the apartment belongs
He's the same dude with the gun
That's one
We have the friend with the cocaine
Two
And another friend I didn't mention
Not through any ill intention
He just didn't say much
As he chose to indulge
Sniffing with him for the joy it would bring
Until the bag had no more for offering
I suppose he makes three
The guy sleeping
Takes us to four
And I did say there was six of us y'know
Her joint was rolled
And it was only me she told
That she was going to smoke
The whiskey we took
As we climbed up to the rooftop
Sat there and smoked on top
I don't know where they thought we got to
But we'd spent many nights on that roof
Cocaine was something we'd done before
And guns weren't something we wanted to see anymore

It seemed like a good point
To head to the roof and share a joint
Talk about love
Speak on peace
Listen to each other
I traded the guns and blow
To listen to what she knows
The weed meant we were good for talking
The whiskey made us not so good for walking
So we stayed the rest of the night out there
To hear the city so quiet was pretty rare

SHOOT

Shoot
Shoot

Shoot a basketball
Shoot me a message
I don't want to shoot at all

Shooting at video games
Shooting at TV screens
Shooting at victims
Shooting at enemies

Shoot
Shoot

Everyone wants to shoot
Shooting guns
Shooting fun
I don't want to shoot at anyone

Shoot to the mall
They sell it all
Shoot to the bank
Shoot to the Walmart
Guns everywhere
Shoot away your cares
I don't want to shoot anywhere

Shoot
Shoot

Shoot all day
Shoot to get paid
Shoot to get laid
I just want to say
I'm tired of everyone shooting each other today

THE GIRL WITH THE CAMERA AT BIG SUR

It was up north at Big Sur
Purple beaches
Mountains
Coastal scenery
No cell reception
Peace
Tranquility
But it wasn't the scenery that particular day
That particular day
I was blown away
By the beauty of the girl with the camera
My lady and I
We were on our way out
We'd both known for a while
But up north we both had to go
She had her friend in tow
We parked up near the beach
They wandered off
I guess we'd all had enough
They'd drifted from my sight
That's when I was drawn to her light
The girl with the camera at Big Sur
Our eyes met
Told a story
Across an empty beach
She said to me
It's okay to be free

I said to her
I didn't expect to find such beauty at Big Sur
Purple beaches
Santa Lucia Mountains
No cell phone reception
And the girl with the camera

FORGOTTEN PEOPLE

Forgotten people
We all come and go
Some are loved by few
Some are loved by more
I was burying a friend at Forest Lawn
Plenty of people there to mourn
His memory will go on
But for just how long?
A time will come
When we're not remembered by anyone
Sure people leave legacies
But it's hard to be
John Lennon
Jack London
Or Muhammed Ali
But eventually
They too
Will fade from memories
As each generation starts to leave
People stop passing down stories
The Saber-tooth came and went
The dodo became extinct
No matter how hard we try
It is certain that we all must die
Maybe our memory will stay alive
At least for a little while
But I do wonder what they'd say

If I dropped dead today
I guess it wouldn't matter to me anyway
Memories tend to quickly fade
Remembered yesterday
Forgotten today
So pour out a double
Let's drink to the forgotten people

THE MASTERPIECE THAT NEVER WAS

The ink in my pen is new
I'm not sure what to do
Figure I'll write nothing but perfekt words
It's what a new pen deserves
Maybe I'll keep writing till she runs out
But I'm about to scream and shout
Make the entire neighborhood wake
I noticed a spelling mistake

All hope is lost

I'm not worth a dime

Life's worthless
Or maybe life's interesting because we're not perfect or perfekt
My faults cut like a knife
But perfection seems to me to be a pretty dull life

ZOMBIES

We're all zombies man
The waking dead
Needing to be watered
Needing to be fed
It was 10pm
Must get to bed
Punch that clock in the morning
Couldn't be late again
At least that's what my boss said
Monday to Friday
Living for the weekend
Keeps the wife happy
And the kids play behind the picket fence
Man
I'm stressed
Boss gave me a new development
We're building apartments
On the cheap
Building on some land
That used to be
Covered in trees
I couldn't believe
This is the man I came to be
When I was a child
I wanted to be a fireman
Fight fires
Save lives

Pick up chicks
What a way to live
In reality fires are hot
And offices are temperature controlled
So my dreams would fold
For an easy paycheck
With ladder climbing opportunities
Metaphorically
Along with corporate impunity
This is our land of the free
I took the kids to the lake
For a nice weekend break
My wife stayed home
To enjoy some time alone
At least that's what she told me
But I saw her put the perfume on
I knew something was going on
She said he was just a friend
But I'd noticed her smiling again
Were these the cards I was dealt?
Or did I pick them myself?
When I was a child
I wanted to be a rock star
Make people sing aloud
Loose women
Fast cars
Now I just wanted to believe her lies
God knows I tried
But the years kept rolling by

And now we sleep in separate houses
My house got smaller
But the profits at work kept getting taller
Then my house got bigger
It was big
Huge
I mean
Holy shit
But the castle was hollow
With no one else to live in it
My children grew up
My daughter's getting her Phd
Some shit with chemistry
And my son is developing property for me
I only wanted them to be happy
I might as well have been a zombie
Walking around dead
On this zombie turning hamster wheel we call life

I'M TAKING THE LAST OF EVERYTHING

I'm taking the last slice of pizza
Taking the final M&M
I'm eating the last chicken wing

I'm tired of not eating
Sick of being hungry
And fed up of putting everyone
And everything
Above me

I'm drinking that last drop of wine
If there's enough coffee in the pot for one
Be sure to pour me one

If I have money in my pocket
I'm the first to share
And people do seem quick to be there
But when money's running low
People tend to change the show

So

I'm eating the last taco
Taking the final chip
And I'm scraping the last bit of dip

I'm tired of being nice
I'm tired of being polite

I'm taking everything in my sight
I'm finishing that bottle tonight
I've got one cigarette that I'm going to light

I'm ready to take the last of everything
Just to take a break from giving everything

I seem to no longer care
So I'll light this here joint
And I'm ready to share

AM I HELPING? AM I HURTING?

Am I helping?
Am I hurting?
I promised to keep you safe
But it's been a while
Since you and I
Went our separate ways
Seemed like things were going okay
But you always did keep a brave face
It was midnight
And you were standing
Out front of my place
I knew you must be desperate
To be standing there so late
I opened a bottle of whiskey
Not a drop went to waste
You didn't want to talk
So we just drank till we couldn't taste
We slept separate
Then you went on your way
But it was a couple of days
And I'd see you again
Am I helping?
Am I hurting?
I promised to keep you safe
Then you told me
Your live-in boyfriend
Just threw the blender through the TV

And you were worried
What the next object would be
And if you were going to become the TV
Y'know metaphorically
You see
I'm actually all about peace
But like most others
Am a victim to my own hypocrisy
Because when you told me this dear
I was filled with fear
Sure he was bigger
According to the picture
I wasn't lying
When I said I'd keep you safe
Or at least die trying
Am I helping?
Am I hurting?
I was trying to distract you
Keep your mind off things
So we went to the Shrine Auditorium
I couldn't believe it too
But magic started happening like it used to do
We were only trying to escape
And sure you needed some space
But we were both taken away
By the melodies
By the bag o' weed
By the sweet whiskey
But we kissed during that song

Do you remember the one
"Take Me Out of the City"
My god
You looked so pretty
Am I helping?
Am I hurting?
It's hard to see past the curtain
The night of the show
You slept on my floor
I said I'd sleep on the couch
You could take the bed
But the words I said
Were useless
To no affect
So I put a pillow beneath your head
Covered you in my duvet
I slept on the couch anyway
I was glad you stayed
But I wondered what he would say
Asked if you needed me to come with you
You said you'd be okay
You dropped some of your things at my place
Then went to some friends out of town to stay
Am I helping?
Am I hurting?
Was at a bar in Echo Park
Had a few glasses of Makers Mark
I was with a few friends
It was long after dark

A guy tapped me on the back
He went on to ask
If I knew your name
I recognized his face
From the picture you showed me
I admit
I could have handled it more diplomatically
Instead I asked him
If he was planning to throw a blender at me
He was not
And quite quickly
After a few punches thrown
He was on top of me
And I was quite seriously
Attempting to get to my feet
I was trapped beneath his gut
As I tried to stand up
He continued to punch
My friend who doesn't happen to give a fuck
Picked up a chair and struck
The prick across the head
He wasn't dead
But there wasn't much movement
So we fled
Am I helping?
Am I hurting?
I promised to keep you safe
It's a promise I want to keep
But I'm starting to think

You're the safest you've been
Ever since I walked away from that scene
I mean
We tried
To make you and I
Us
So many times
It's obscene
Maybe we're best in each other's memories
I only hope that sometimes you remember me
I always tried to do
What I thought was best
But it always seemed impossible
Impossible to tell for certain
If I ever was helping
Or if I only ever was hurting

LIVIN' TURNS TO DYIN'

I didn't really care who I hurt
As long as there were more people laughing than those who weren't
Bridges burned
Friendships turned
I never learned
I was always a moth to a flame
Constantly looking for ways to start again
Completely insane
Rattled with pain
Forgetting my name
Always trying to break new ground
Not listening to anyone around
Nothing profound
Forgotten sound
Nowhere bound
I keep travelling on
Wondering where it all went wrong
A played out song
A solo sing-a-long
A weed-less bong
I just don't know where to go anymore
I'm tired of being yesterday's whore
Breaking laws
Dropping jaws
A meaningless cause
I could have been a better man

But I keep doing what I can
Hope you understand
I am who I am
Goddamn
I'll keep on trying
But trying sounds a lot like lying
I'm not selling nor am I buying
I'm clarifying
And it's satisfying
But terrifying
Eventually living turns to dying

THE ONLY ADVICE I EVER LISTENED TO

They say don't act on your thinking
If you've been out drinking
Your thoughts become ghoulish
And you may be prone to act foolish
I don't normally take advice
But I took some twice
First bit of advice
And I hope you're listening to this
Don't eat the nuts in the barroom
They're covered in piss
Second piece of advice
If you're down and life seems hopeless
You are completely stressed
Maybe depressed
And life is seeming far from its best
You might be in the funkiest of funks
Just don't make permanent decisions when you're drunk
Dying is kind of a one-time deal
Sometimes living creates feelings that become too hard to feel
But no matter how hard life gets
Those two pieces of advice have me convinced
I was standing on the ledge
I didn't jump but I haven't sobered up since
I've drank my share of shitty beers
And a few fine wines
Maybe I'm dying or maybe I'm buying time

What does it matter anyway
The world is completely insane

There's piss on bar snacks for fuck's sake

THIS IS NOT A TEST

If I step outside
I'm sure to find lovers
Walking the streets
Holding hands with one another
I want to stay inside
And hide under the covers
Sure we sleep when we're dead
But a casket isn't a bed

Life is wasted on the living
Death is lost on the rest
This is not a test
Grudges are unforgiving
Life doesn't provide us with bulletproof vests
I repeat
This is not a test

I don't know why
But I can't find the words to say
I've been lying to myself
Saying everything's okay
Sometimes truth causes pain
But it's too late to speak it from the grave
I love you baby
But I couldn't ask you to save me

Life is wasted on the living
Death is lost on the rest
This is not a test
It's hard to keep giving
When you're far from your best
I repeat
This is not a test

I'm tired of working all hours of the day
Can't remember my last vacation
I show up at nine and I leave right at five
Sure I'm alive but I'm complaining for the duration
My friends want to meet
But I refuse their invitation
I'm just so tired
Of doing more than what's required

Life is wasted on the living
Death is lost on the rest
This is not a test
Sometimes the joy remains hidden
But I need a rest
I repeat
This is not a test

Today is all that is certain
So why do we wait?
No more time to waste
Taking the preacher's bait

Promised eternity in heaven
As long as I dedicate
My only life to a lie
Yet people still try

Life is wasted on the living
Death is lost on the rest
This is not a test
Plus God's supposed to be forgiving
So if I'm wrong I might still be blessed
I repeat
This life's not a test

GOOD NEWS FOR THE BAD NEWS BLUES

I have good news
Good news
For those of you
That enjoy the bad news blues
Because I have something to say
Everything is okay
In a not okay
Sort of way
So
Everything is not okay
In an okay
Sort of way
I woke up today
That was okay
My head didn't feel great
And whiskey I could still taste
So it wasn't all okay
But I was awake
I could hear my friend in the kitchen
I could smell the coffee
That he laid out for me
On the table next to where I was asleep
It was a coffee table
And I was barely able
But I managed to pull myself upright on the couch
Moved the cushions about
And gave my friend a shout

He told me not to be too loud
His girlfriend was asleep
They'd drank some wine the previous night
While watching a movie
He said he guessed I found the key
I told him I did
And I let myself in
Asked if I was planning to stay
But I had to be on my way
Wondered where I was planning to stay
Told him I had a place
A girl I knew out Venice way
Said she was going away
For just two days
But apparently cats don't fuck with a suitcase
So the cat stayed
Sure I'm allergic
But it meant I had a place to stay
Everything was okay
In a not okay sort of way
I was supposed to be
At this bar by three
A bar on Abbot Kinney
That's where she left me
Her apartment key
She was working
Tending bar till it was time for her to leave
So I walk down
To the redline

Over on Hollywood and Vine
To meet a friend of mine
At Union Station which was fine
Because he was planning to drive
Over to the Westside
After picking up a friend coming in from Irvine
They were due to arrive
At 12:49
So I thought I might as well catch a ride
Because the friend lives out west
Just near Venice
Seemed to work out for the best
What a coincidence
Everything was okay
But in a not okay sort of way
You see
The train was delayed
My friend's friend was running late
I thought I should wait
But I too was starting to run late
And I knew my friend
Did intend
To leave exactly at three
So I hopped the redline
The purple line
And then the E
Finishing up on the 733
Took me an hour thirty
Everything wasn't how it was supposed to be

Although I got the chance to read a short story
As I tried to get to where I needed to be
The story was a little bleak
But it certainly did seem to speak to me
Because although everything was okay
It was okay in a very not okay sort of way
I can't remember the author's name
But the story received its own kind of fame
Called it *Quinta Del Sordo*
In Venice I did arrive
I made it just in time
She gave me a note with instructions on
Told me to call if anything goes wrong
I said "I don't need no instructions to feed a damn cat"
She wasn't quite happy with that
Told me to read them so I did
And man
That cat knew how to live
Ate more meals a day than me
So she poured me a whiskey
Told me it was free
Then gave me her key
Everything was okay
In a not okay sort of way
You see
She gave me a key
To her apartment door
But there's another door you have to go through before
And that door

She didn't give me a key for
But everything was okay
Just in a not okay sort of way
I didn't realize until pretty late
Because the first time I went back
To feed the damn cat
Some guy held the door for me
So I didn't know I needed a different key
My friend was drinking down the street
He asked me if I wanted to meet
We drank till we lost our feet
He took a cab
I walked back in the ocean breeze
Life ain't cheap
And good times are seldom free
Although they have been known to be
I didn't know where I'd sleep
When I saw time had turned to the next 3
Not afternoon 3
But 3am in the morning
When the realization was dawning
I needed another key
Everything was not okay
But in an okay sort of way
Because past the side gate
Was the back door which was usually unlocked
So the gate I hopped
But then I stopped
The door was locked

But the door was old as fuck
So I thought I could pick the lock
I could not
So I sat down wondering what to do
I was feeling a case of the bad news blues
Eventually I fell asleep
To be awoken by the police
Prodding at me
With their sticks
Couple of dicks
Asked me why
Why I was asleep outside
I told them I left my key inside
Had too much pride
To wake up my neighbors
They said it didn't seem like believable or acceptable behavior
At that moment someone opened the door
Someone I'd never seen before
Maybe he'd seen me
Or maybe he just hated LAPD
Both are quite likely
And a genuine possibility
But he decided to vouch for me
They had good news for me
As they let me walk free
So I told my new friend to "have a good evening"
He told me to "have a good night"
But I got a fright

When the cat was nowhere in sight
I'd turned on all the lights
Then I saw it asleep on my pillow
I'm sure the cat did know
I was allergic and had a pretty long day
Everything was okay
In a not okay sort of way
I woke up sneezing
And I woke up coughing
The cat woke up like I meant nothing
And I had to feed the damn thing
I read the instructions on the list
The ungrateful bastard hissed
And I'm not proud of this
But I was a little pissed
So I clenched my fists
And right back at the cat I hissed
The cat turned up its nose and I was dismissed
I didn't want to leave
Until late in the eve
Past the cat's final feeding time
So I drank myself a bottle of wine
Called up an old friend of mine
And when I say friend
I'd be lying
If I were to say we hadn't slept together
Come to think of it
That's all we did
Who am I to kid

We became romantic
But I quickly hid
Like a scared little child
Heartbroken and fragile
Is how I felt for a while
But she made me smile
She was a little wild
She'd already had a divorce filed
Was once charged with assault
It wasn't her fault
The cops pulled her over for driving too fast
She'd had an interesting past
And the die seemed to be cast
They wanted to do a breathalyzer test
She was a little stressed
Calling them dicks to their faces probably wasn't the best idea
But she never had any fear
She was also pretty hot
Let's just be clear
Could have probably got away with that
Then she called one officer fat
And in the other officer's face she spat
Then she was grabbed
Not before the officer was jabbed
With that sweet left hand
But she always seemed to understand
That life always seems to have its demands
In its own sort of way
Everything is okay

In a not okay
Sort of way
She picked me up in her car
To drive back over to the Eastside
Where she did reside
We talked on how we tried
Neither of us lied
And our secrets we always could confide
But occasionally she'd get lost in my arms
And I'd end in hers
But no-one was left to care
We were just happy to be there
It was all okay
In a not okay
Sort of way
None of that was new
I'm no stranger to
The *in between places walking around Los Angeles blues*
I had so many places I could go
But into her arms I fell
Sure me and her could continue to turn heaven to hell
But we'd been drinking from the well
At least until
We felt
Everything is okay
In a not okay
Sort of way
I caught a case
And I hear its good news
Good News for the Bad News Blues

QUINTA DEL SORDO A SHORT STORY BY JOHNNY SNYDER

I was obsessed with death for as long as I could remember, like a love-sick puppy I followed it around. I read stories in newspapers that scared me senseless but I could never help but to keep reading out of some twisted morbid curiosity. I watched movies that were beyond my years, men on violent killing sprees normally to carry out some vigilante justice. A brave protagonist who kills a lot of people and is treated as a hero. The mixed messages of the world filtered through my ears, beyond my skull and rested firmly in my brain. As I began to grow older my fascination didn't decrease. It intensified. I grew transfixed by the mystery.

People die every day. Babies are born every day and one day they will die too, it is the only certainty in life. Death ties us together as humans, we can all connect with the concept of death yet we can never truly understand it until we are wrapped in her cold embrace.

I haven't left my house in two months. Three months ago life was different. I worked a decent job. I looked presentable, I even wore a suit on occasion, my hair was short, my face clean, my body was slim yet muscular. Currently none of those things apply to me. Not because I suffered some horrific misfortune, I didn't. My girlfriend didn't break up with me, my wife didn't leave, my kids didn't kill anybody, I wasn't abused or beaten. I've never had children, I'm single and I have suffered no major trauma recently. I simply decided to lock my door because the world beyond the door was not a place I wanted to inhabit anymore, yet the doubt about what is beyond this universe outweighed the desire to end my life.

My beard hangs beneath my chin, covering my throat, my hair is unwashed and greasy, my dressing gown has various marks on it where I have perhaps spilt food or drink. I wear loosely fitted underwear beneath my robe and no t-shirt.

The walls are grey, a painting hangs above an old television screen, Francisco Goya, *Saturno devorando a un hijo*. I stare at it intently from a seated position on my worn burgundy couch. I used to fraternize with the people beyond my walls but I was always left empty and unfulfilled. I saw women as visions of beauty and couldn't help falling lovesick at the slightest smile. I was a romantic at heart but after enough failed attempts I realized that my path had to change.

People may try to label me as agoraphobic but I'm not, I might be called paranoid, delusional or insane. My curtains are tightly closed, there is not a single flicker of light. The television remains turned off as it only ever seems to contain nonsense. I have shelves that are packed with books and a layer of dust lie on each one. The words appear insignificant and weak.

I didn't wake up one morning and suddenly decide to lock my doors, a split moment decision like that could be considered an act of lunacy. I planned for weeks, I bought food and water in bulk. I forwarded my post to the address of my old job as they didn't have my current contact details. I didn't wish to be disturbed as I built my own universe within the confines of my modest home. Every neighbour I cordially uttered the words 'hello' to in the past, fill the pit of my stomach with a wretched sickness. My family who have all moved on make me react the same, as they revel in their lavish lifestyles. The locals in the pub at the end of my gloomy street force me to scroll through my mind as my imagination contemplates a very slow and painful death for each of them. There is no particular personal reason for such vivid, vile animosity. I hate the mundane conversations about endless garbage that is deemed acceptable. Anecdotes and opinions in this modern world seem to pollute my mind with a toxic curse. Talk about reality television, pop songs, how much each other can drink, topics that progress with age to hospital appointments, holidays and fine wines. Each topic as meaningless as the next and I wish them dead a million times over. They will not ruin my new world.

I don't wish to be God. Whether he exists or not. However, when the world discusses the most twisted minds in history, Jack the Ripper, Charles Manson, John Wayne Gacy, Adolf Hitler, all are responsible for acts of intolerable cruelty. Yet God sent his own Son to die in the most horrific way imaginable and He is a hero? It's a mixed message. Or perhaps I cannot trust my own brain anymore. I possibly locked myself in as much as I locked the world out.

I stand from my couch and walk slowly to my kitchen. Empty boxes of cereal are stacked by my back door, empty packets of crisps, empty tins of beans, peas and corn. Empty containers lie cluttering my kitchen into disbelief. God created the world in seven days, it may take me longer but I have nowhere to go. I rummage through a number of drawers until I find them, an old pair of scissors. I pick up the first box of cereal and cut the lid off. I stand it on the floor and slowly cut an even number of squares in the side of the box to replicate windows. I have completed my first building. I have a couple of scraps left over. I shape them into two-dimensional people. I stand my first person against the doorway of my new building.

I no longer subscribe to any human traditions, I sleep when I want, I eat when I wish, there are no clocks in my home therefore I am unaware of time, I am incapable of guessing the day. I now live by my own rules. My city is taking shape, it has been weeks since I began the building process. I have roads fitted in between buildings. Some buildings are tall and some small. I have now pushed my couch against the window in an attempt to allow my project to develop. I have cut tin cans in half so that my people made from cardboard have their own transportation, I would hate to make them dependent. There is little worse than a mind that is governed by other people's thoughts. I used to hear the word freedom hurled around loosely. I have never met someone that has exercised the right to be free. We are controlled by everybody we interact with, we wish to be accepted, loved and appreciated by other humans who lack the necessary qualifications to extend such generosities. Our only breath of true freedom is our last one. I have never felt that sweet release of air push against my face from the mouth of another. I can't say for certain that I will have the clarity to appreciate my last breath.

The inevitability of my life ending drives me to keep creating my design, we all wish to leave a lasting memory, a legacy, it is perhaps a flaw. My life's worth is the journey to becoming a God within my own darkness.

I cut my newest character out of a small box of chocolates I buried away some time ago. She is sweet, delicate and beautiful. I place her on the top of my tallest building so that she has the greatest view. I shouldn't have favourites considering my position of power, but she has a kind body, her face is blurred but her personality shines brighter than anything, I will impress her as she watches me complete my construction. A week passes and she refuses to look at me. It's not good enough. I am not moving fast enough, multiple buildings and roads and cars are being created daily, the population is growing but my steady pace is ungodly. I ask for her hand but she refuses. I continue my quest another week. Her heart isn't as cold, I feel the warmth of her body at my fingertips. I can't move unrecognized in this world anymore. It is too grand. It is complete. An entire city within my walls. She asks me silently where she will live. I have plenty of homes. A house for every citizen. Her home is much more special. I take her upstairs to my room of rest so she can see the heaven above. How large everything is in comparison to the city downstairs. She is overwhelmed, almost too shocked, dangerously shocked. I walk her back, and tell her she will live there once her mortal life is over. We develop our relationship, she watches as I eat. Occasionally she will visit me in my sleep, her body will dance with the weight of my breath. Her eyes never wander.

I begin to forget about my creation and in time it begins to dismantle itself. People fall to the ground, buildings crumble in my neglect. I am weak and in love. My city that I loved so much now disgusts me like the world I once knew. I raise my foot high above my tallest office block and I crush it with my foot, I see figures jumping out of windows. I feel the glare of my love as she looks on with disbelief. I whisper in her ear with a tear dripping down my face 'it's time to live where I promised you' I hear her response 'heaven?' At that, I place her head in my mouth and I bite down viciously, the roof of my mouth is shot with an indescribable puff of air. The final breath I longed for my entire life. I kick and I punch every little item I ever touched or built. It is a cleansing flood. I am sweating, hysterical, wailing at the moon. This is my house of death. Casa de la mort.

GOOD NEWS FOR THE BAD NEWS BLUES CONTINUED

I told you the story was a little bleak
It was about a guy not going outside for weeks
Maybe that was the opposite to me
But we don't need to be the same
For words to speak
And those words spoke to me
Gently
I woke on the Eastside
Where this girl did reside
I was waking in her bed
Next to empty bottles of wine
But everything was fine
We kept our clothes on that particular time
Talking into the early hours
About how sweetness can turn sour
We sat on her rooftop
It may have only been a few stories high
But we felt like we were sat on a tower
She let me use the shower
We had a coffee and waited around
Till I needed to catch the train downtown
In Hollywood you always have to meet some dude
Those dudes
They know other dudes
I'm not trying to be funny
But you meet these dudes
To get to the dude with the money

That dude
Takes a look at the art you do
Says it sounds really cool
Takes a day or two
Then gets his people to get back to you
Saying the man with the money loves what you do
He just doesn't think it's the perfect fit
And to talk quite frankly
And to speak quite blankly
There isn't much money in poetry
I think to myself
No shit
But I keep doing it
So I arrived at this bar
Where one of those meetings was planned
Called the bar *Seven Grand*
There were some dudes in suits
A few women too
I sat down in a booth
With a Bookers 130 proof
A Bourbon I couldn't afford
Staring out at the door
My glass is empty so I order one more
Clock went from three o'clock
Turned itself into four
I still sat alone
So I got the bartender to pour
Once more
Waiting seemed bad for my health

And was not good for my prospects of wealth
But all was okay
I decided to play
A game of pool by myself
I won
I also lost
I didn't want to know how much a good time costs
In a place like that
So I ordered another double shot
Before I gave up on the clock
I received a message to say
Apologies for the delay
But it was the dude asking me if we can meet another day
I didn't think that was okay
But I was feeling good enough to say
Everything is okay
In a fucked up sort of way
I wasn't going to pay another dime
So I went outside
In order to find
A cheaper place to think
A less pretentious kind of drink
I see this Irish bar down the street
Looks like more of a fun place to be
There was a chick fighting with security
She was wearing tall black heels
And some slim black lingerie
She was like a menagerie
She must have been having some kind of day

She sure did have a lot to say
I wondered where she'd go
And if she'd let me tag along
But I've met women like that before
Everything is great
Till it's not
Then you're hiding from her best shots
And love becomes something you both forgot
So I thought I was safer
To drink in the bar she was coming from
Instead of the bar that was a little farther along
Because that was likely to be the next lyric of her song
And a few more drinks
Might be all it takes
For my mistakes
To make
It all go wrong
I got a call from a friend
He said he was at a loose end
So I told him to come on by
We talked of work
We talked on friends
On women
On regrets
And on love
You know
The type of talk that happens on barstools
Drinking beer
Drinking whiskey

Drinking rye
I mentioned a long time ago
Long before I started to write these words
That I'd been giving a friend
A few bucks to pay some rent
But I hadn't been to his place in a while
Since a few guys across the way
Had a few choice words to say
Those words happened to be pointed my way
Told me I should find somewhere else to stay
Or they'd put me away
But it's hard to explain
With a gun in your face
I was told low is how I must lay
Until this case
Of mistaken identity is cleared away
But everything was cool
Just in a not so cool
Kind of way
Last orders were called
We were walking south long after dark
About 15 blocks south of MacArthur Park
With still a few blocks to go
I could hear a few sirens in the distance
Which is not at all unusual to hear
The sirens started to become more clear
As this little white car speeds past
He was going pretty fast
There were three police cars in pursuit

Doing what police cars sometimes do
But this little white car really flew
He seemed to have the beating on those few
That continued to follow
As they drove out of sight
Could hear them no more
I was wondering if he was okay
As we continued to my friend's place
I heard some more sirens in the distance
I saw the little white car reaching full speed
The one being chased by the police
I don't know where he'd been
But he turned and made his way back to the way he came
He was really trying to stay free
But the officers seemed quite keen
First there were three police cars
But on the way back I counted fifteen
And a helicopter
Whatever was happening in that guy's day
Certainly didn't seem okay
In any kind of way
We made it back to outside my friend's place
Said the air mattress was still on the floor
But he didn't know if it had any air any more
That's when we saw the guy that got in my face
You remember the one?
The man with the gun
He asked me if he could have a cigarette
I said okay

He asked then if I smoked
So I knew he meant smoking in a different way
I told him I smoke most days
He said he was about to light a blunt
If I cared to partake
I did hesitate
As I asked "do you remember the gun thing?"
He nodded
I continued "so are we cool?"
He said "I just offered you a blunt
Fool"
I thought he made a very good point
So my friend passed him the fifth of whiskey
We shared on the walk
We sipped
We smoked
We spoke
My new friend asked why I came back around
I told him this isn't the town
For people that are scared to lose
I had the *in between places walking around Los Angeles Blues*
That's when he passed me the good news
And everything was okay
And I am here to say
Everything is okay
In a not okay
Sort of way
Sometimes the *Bad News Blues*
Can bring some *Good News* too

THE END

www.ingramcontent.com/pod-product-compliance
Lightning Source LLC
LaVergne TN
LVHW041045080426
835508LV00036B/911